Couple Talk

How to Talk Your Way to a Great Relationship

Chick Moorman
Thomas Haller

Personal Power Press
Merrill, MI

Couple Talk

How to Talk Your Way to a Great Relationship

Library of Congress Catalogue Card Number
2003094097

ISBN 0-9616046-6-2

Personal Power Press
P.O. Box 547
Merrill, MI 48637

COVER DESIGN
Foster & Foster, Inc.
www.fostercovers.com

BOOK DESIGN
Tagline Communications, Inc.
www.tagline.com

TABLE OF CONTENTS

INTRODUCTION

COUPLES OFTEN FIND THEMSELVES struggling to communicate. You say one thing; your partner hears another. You have a vague sense that your partner wants to say something, but she remains silent. You want to be told directly; your partner seems to be dancing around an issue. You want to send a clean message, yet you hear yourself say something that reminds you of how your mother talked to your father. Verbal communication is fraught with the potential for misinterpretation and misunderstanding. An undeniable link exists between the words you choose to use and the emotional health and well-being of your relationship.

The book you hold in your hands offers a variety of verbal skills and language patterns that can strengthen your primary relationship by improving communication between you and your partner. By carefully choosing words and phrases that communicate love and respect and by expressing them honestly and openly, you can build a relationship based on mutual respect and caring.

Couple Talk invites you to examine your language patterns to see if your style of communication is creating what you want in your relationship. It offers you verbal tools that you can put to use immediately to strengthen your partnership. It will help you become a *response-able* communicator—able to respond appropriately and effectively to the everyday situations that all couples encounter. To that end, we suggest specific signature phrases and language strategies that create a culture of honesty, caring, respect, and intimacy in your relationship. We also recommend the elimination of certain words and phrases from your Couple Talk repertoire—ways of speaking that we believe ignore feelings, show disrespect, create distance, and invite codependence.

The first chapter, "The Language of Listening and Understanding," suggests language that invites your partner to talk while you assume the listening stance. It will help you construct questions that encourage more than a one-word response, speak in ways that allow you to "demonstrate" understanding rather than simply stating that you understand, and introduce potentially hurtful issues in language that invites discussion and communication rather than shuts it down.

The next chapter, "The Language of Feelings," is an effort to help you communicate feelings honestly, openly, and directly. It shows you how to use language that claims ownership of your feelings without assigning responsibility for them to your partner or some other external source. You will learn the Describe/Describe/Describe technique for communicating anger, frustration, or irritation without wounding your partner's spirit or attacking his or her personality.

"The Language of Intimacy" focuses on ways to communicate love and acceptance, including how to ask for what you want while maintaining closeness, warmth, and connectedness.

"The Language of Solution-Seeking" concerns itself primarily with problem-solving: how to focus on one complaint at a time, take appropriate time-outs, and find ways for both you and your partner to get what you want.

"The Language of Respect" and "The Language of Disrespect" are parallel chapters that will help you discern the difference between words that communicate appreciation and those that invite shame. In these chapters you will have an opportunity to find out if you or your partner has a need to be right or if you tease inappropriately. You will learn why the language of luck, mental scorekeeping, and advice-giving sabotages relationships. You will also discover if either you or your partner use words that suggest verbal abuse may be occurring.

The next chapter, "The Language of Boundaries," will help you draw clear lines, communicate when your boundaries are being violated, respectfully tell your partner to back off, and take care of yourself when necessary.

"The Language of Autonomy" describes how to use words that give your partner space to make his or her own decisions, solve their own problems, and accept help when they are ready. It covers ways to invite independence in your partner and to request autonomy for yourself.

The final chapter, "The Language of Behavioral Change," will help you learn verbal skills for requesting a change of behavior from your partner; for responding to attempts at behavior change; for excuse giving; and for disowning responsibility for present actions. You will also learn how to make a "Be" choice, how to communicate to your partner that sincere words need to be accompanied by appropriate actions, and why "trying" doesn't work.

On the pages that follow you will be exposed to words and phrases that may confront your current behavior and challenge your present communication style. What you choose to take from these pages is your decision. How you decide to use these techniques is also your choice.

Couple Talk has been designed to help you increase the number of verbal tools you have available in your partnering toolbox. With an increased variety of verbal tools at your disposal, you increase the likelihood that you and your partner will match the most effective tool to the appropriate situation.

Having the right tools at your disposal is a helpful start, but the truth is, having a full toolbox by itself is not enough. To become an effective communicator and a valuable partner, you must put the tools to use. Regularly. No one becomes a proficient typist overnight. No one learns a foreign language without practicing consistently. The skills work if you work at using the skills.

Be advised that there is no one phrase, no single set of words, which will immediately transform your relationship or your communication patterns. This book teaches a style of language and a system of communication that, with consistent use, will have a cumulative effect. Repetition is critical. Repeated use of these verbal skills, delivered from an open heart with a loving attitude, will eventually produce a more open, honest, and respectful pattern of communication between you and your partner.

Your attitude is important. Just mouthing the words is not enough. Simply using new language without an accompanying attitude of love and respect will have little impact. A child who puts on his father's shoes and walks around the room using the same words his father uses does not magically become a dad. Likewise, if you and your partner walk around your home mouthing these techniques without intentions of closeness and appreciation, you will not likely connect as a couple. Effective Couple Talk needs to be linked with loving intentions and a respectful attitude.

A word of warning about what this book is not. It is not about keeping you and your partner together as a couple. We have no vested interest in whether or not you continue as partners or decide to move in separate directions. The length of a relationship is not the full measure of its success. A successful relationship is one in which the partners grow both individually and collectively and in which each supports the other in becoming fully who and what they want to be for as long as they are together. Our goal is to help you create an environment that supports the growth of both you and your partner whether you stay together for three months or for thirty years.

Couple Talk is also not an attempt to provide therapy. It is a skill-based system of verbal strategies designed to improve relationships through effective communication. Our intent is to provide you with the essential verbal ingredients to create a loving, respectful relationship with the partner of your choice, one that is held firmly together with trust, caring, and compassion.

The Couple Talk phrases presented on the pages that follow can be used in a variety of relationships: with your spouse, your fiancé, or a person you have known for only two weeks; with your parents, your sister, or your boss; with colleagues, neighbors, or a trusted mentor. They work with partnerships of the same sex and with those of the opposite sex. They work with those who fall above you or below you on the corporate ladder.

If you and your partner are using the material in this book together, great! You will both be able to recognize a phrase or technique when it is used and will understand what the other is attempting to communicate. If, however, your partner is not reading this book along with you, the phrases will still be a valuable verbal tool in fostering relationship. Each is presented in a way that explains how it can benefit you directly, here and now, with or without your partner's conscious involvement.

You will notice that we have also included a "Hearing" section for each phrase. <u>While you cannot control how your partner talks to you—what he or she says and the tone of voice he or she uses—*you* are in control of how you interpret what you hear.</u> We provide specific suggestions for how to hear and interpret your partner's words in a way that true communication can occur and connection can be maintained.

The phrases and suggestions in *Couple Talk* are products of what we have learned in our roles as partner, spouse, psychotherapist, educator, mentor, sibling, and friend—some from personal experience and some from observing others in relationship. Much of it we have used successfully in therapy sessions and in workshop presentations. Some of it came easily. Some we learned the hard way.

We do not present this material from the perspective of experts who have mastered the art of effective communication. Our own personal relationships reflect ups and downs, struggles and successes. Our goal for ourselves is to move steadily toward making those relationships mutually satisfying and emotionally healthy.

We invite you to join us.

CHAPTER I

The Language
of Listening
and Understanding

"Say some more."

"I'M NOT HAPPY with our sex life," Kevin announced at the beginning of a scheduled problem-solving meeting with his wife. "It's getting boring for me. I feel like I have to hold back my feelings of lust and pretend that all I feel is sweetness and love. I want to get a bit earthier—let the wild man part of me surface more often." He paused and looked sheepishly at his wife of seven years to check her reaction. "Say some more," she suggested.

Kevin took a breath and continued. His wife, Marilyn, leaned forward, demonstrating her willingness to hear whatever Kevin wanted to say. She made strong eye contact and did not interrupt his narrative.

Marilyn's desire to speak during Kevin's disclosure was strong. She wanted to defend herself. She wanted to tell her side of the story. She wanted to express her needs. But she controlled her desire to interrupt her spouse because she suspected he had a strong need to talk. And she wanted to hear what he had to say. She knew it was important for him to say it. And she knew it was important for her to hear it.

"Say some more" is Couple Talk that signals your partner that it is still his turn. It gives him permission to keep talking. It informs him that you care more about listening and understanding at this moment than you do about getting across your point of view.

"Say some more" does not mean that you have nothing to say. It does not mean that you don't want a turn. It means that you are willing to delay your response until you're sure your partner has finished. It means you're willing to take your turn later, after you have fully heard and understood all that he has to say. Other phrases that invite your partner to say more include:

"Go on."

"Please continue."

"Keep it rolling."

"Let me hear all of it."

"Keep talking."

"It's still your turn."

When your partner excitedly tells you about her eventful day, asking her to keep talking will give her permission to expand on her ideas and feelings. "It's still your turn" is one way to signal that it's OK for her to continue to vent. "Please continue" is an invitation to keep sharing her strong feelings of frustration, irritation, or anger.

Use "Say some more" or one of the variations listed above whenever you feel it is important for your partner to keep talking. Once you fully hear what he or she has to say, you will be better able to respond appropriately and effectively.

HEARING

"Say some more" means that your spouse wants to hear all of what you have to say. He or she is willing to listen while you continue talking. Trust their communication. Say more. Be assured that they will take their turn later. When they do, let them speak until they stop talking. Then say, "Please continue."

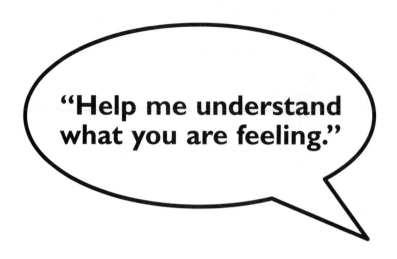

"Help me understand what you are feeling."

SANDY CAME HOME from work and found her husband, Mark, sitting on the couch staring at a blank television set. She knew immediately that something was wrong. Mark looked like he was about to cry. His face reflected pain, hurt, and sadness.

Sandy's mind filled with questions. What could be the problem? What happened? Did she do something? What could she do to help? Should she hold him or leave him alone? Should she go over and sit with him? Should she call his boss to find out what happened?

She wasn't sure what to do, but she wanted to do something. She took a deep breath and tried to relax. At that moment, she recalled a phrase that she had learned several months earlier at a Couple Talk partnering workshop. With a calm voice she said, "Help me understand what you are feeling."

"I don't know," Mark replied. "I just feel blah."

Sandy persisted. "Help me understand what 'blah' is like for you. Does it seem flat, sad, ugly, or what? Describe it to me."

For the next hour Sandy sat and listened. Periodically, she asked a question to gain a deeper understanding. She didn't attempt to fix things. She didn't try to change anything. She simply sat there, being available for her husband, opening herself to receive whatever he was ready to offer. Slowly, with the help of a partner who sincerely wanted to understand, Mark began to identify and express his feelings.

Sandy successfully avoided the trap that many spouses fall into—the "I've got to fix it" trap. We think that if we could just do the right thing our spouse would feel better. We're not sure what the right thing is, so we adopt a hit and miss approach, guessing at what he or she needs and hoping to hit it.

The strength of your relationship is not based on your ability to fix, alter, or change situations that your partner faces. Connectedness in relationships springs from understanding, acceptance, and a willingness to receive new thoughts and feelings from each other.

Sandy put her desire to fix on hold and opted instead to seek an understanding of what Mark was thinking and feeling. "Help me understand what you are feeling" is a way to stop playing fixer and psychic. It changes the goal from fixing to understanding. It helps you assume the posture of receiving. It tells your partner: Your feelings are important to me. I'm ready to listen.

Do not equate "fixing" with "doing" and "not fixing" with "not doing." Sandy chose not to try to fix the situation, but she did choose to do something. She chose to listen, receive, accept, clarify, and question. She received her husband's thoughts and feelings, accepted them, and allowed Mark to be whoever he needed to be at that moment. She stayed connected.

HEARING

When your partner says, "Help me understand what you are feeling," hear it as her attempt to stay open to your needs. Communicate. The silent treatment won't work here. If what you need in that moment is time and space alone, then say that. Give her a chance to honor that need without feeling shut out. Later, when you're ready, you can communicate your thoughts and feelings in a way that helps her understand them and you.

"I UNDERSTAND just how you feel" is Couple Talk that attempts to communicate: I know what it's like for you. I've been there, too. I understand. But regardless of the sincerity with which the phrase is delivered, it is not true. No one can understand exactly how another person feels. No two people have the exact same experience, nor is their perception of their experience the same. Even partners who have been together over half a century have unique interpretations of the same events. In truth, we are all different, and so is our experience of life.

When your partner is caught up in strong emotion, it is not time to tell her you understand; it is time to *demonstrate* that you understand. Active listening is a technique that will help you do that.

In order to listen actively you must first be quiet. Assume the listening stance by attending with your body. Make strong eye contact and assume an open body posture. Do not interrupt the narrative. When *NOTE* your partner stops talking, paraphrase what you heard and saw. State the feeling and a possible reason: "You feel _____ because _____."

If your spouse tells you she's mad because she was publicly corrected at work, do not presume that you understand. Remember, *demonstrating* understanding is more useful than *saying* that you understand. Use a reflective response to check out the accuracy of your understanding. Do not use your spouse's exact words. Paraphrase them. Say, for instance, "You're angry because your boss made an example of you in front of your colleagues," or "You're mad at your boss for reprimanding you in public rather than in private."

If your words accurately reflect your partner's feelings, he or she will likely acknowledge your understanding by continuing the dialogue, blowing off steam, and giving you more information. Again, use active listening by rephrasing their message as you reflect their feelings and concerns back to them. Remember, you are simply listening. This is not a time to give advice or soothe feelings. Just listen actively.

If your initial paraphrase is inaccurate, your partner can correct the misconception by restating or embellishing their original comments. Either way you arrive at a position of understanding.

When your partner shares her reaction to not receiving a birthday card from her brother, refrain from saying, "I know what that's like," even though you have vivid memories of having your birthday pass unacknowledged by a former girlfriend. Instead, reflect her feelings and concerns in your own words. "You feel sad because no card came from your brother," or "It's bumming you out that your brother forgot your birthday again."

It is unnecessary and unproductive to give advice by telling your partner that she shouldn't feel bad or that she'll get over it. All you need to do is to listen skillfully. She will feel comforted and supported simply because she feels understood.

Reflective listening is an act of respect. It informs your partner: I don't presume to know exactly how you feel, but I'm ready to listen and I want to understand. I'm willing to check it out and see if I understand it correctly. You are worth my time and energy.

As you practice, your active listening skills will improve. As they grow, you will notice that your relationship with your partner is growing as well. Relationships improve when partners demonstrate over time that they really do care about the other's feelings and concerns.

HEARING

If you hear your partner saying things like, "You sound frustrated with your boss" or "That tight schedule is creating a lot of stress for you right now," know that he or she is working hard to understand your feelings. If it sounds to you like you're being "techniqued," hear that your partner cares enough about you and your concerns to risk practicing a strategy designed to help strengthen your relationship. Hear more than an unskillful attempt; hear the effort and the willingness to learn and the concern for you that is behind the use of what may sound like a technique.

If you recognize an attempt to paraphrase, whether skillful or crude, give your partner some feedback. If he says, "You're angry because the mechanic didn't tell you everything the first time" and the paraphrase is accurate, say, "You got it," or "That's right," or simply, "Yes." If the paraphrase is off base, correct it. Tell him, "No, I'm frustrated because it cost so much money," if that is what's true for you.

As your partner gets more skillful with active listening, your feelings of connectedness will grow. So will the number of times you go to him for listening.

TEN THINGS TO SAY TO HELP YOUR PARTNER FEEL HEARD

1. "I'm listening."

2. "Tell me more about that."

3. "Help me understand your perspective."

4. "Talk slower. I'm trying to process all that you're saying."

5. "How does that affect how you feel?"

6. "I'm missing something. Can you tell me again?"

7. "What are some possible solutions that you've thought of?"

8. "Let me turn off the TV before you start telling me."

9. "I want to hear what you have to say."

10. "Let's talk about this when there aren't so many distractions."

"Is there something up with you?"

SHARON AND BUTCH took ballroom dance lessons together every Sunday night. They were introduced to each other in a dance class and continued the activity throughout their courtship and on into marriage.

During one Sunday night lesson Butch noticed that Sharon wasn't responding to his cues the way she usually did. She seemed preoccupied and wasn't following his lead consistently. She seemed to be somewhere else. Butch suspected that something was bothering her.

He took his wife by the hand and led her off the dance floor into the privacy of the hall. "I have a sense that you're not really here tonight," he began. "Is there something up with you?" Sharon dropped her head and stared at the floor, a sure sign that Butch had hit a nerve. "What's going on?" he asked in a tone that indicated genuine concern.

"I feel like you're forcing me with your leading tonight," Sharon responded. "I like to be led, not forced."

Butch's inquiry and Sharon's willingness to give him the information he needed led to an eight-minute conversation that clarified the situation and resolved the problem for both of them. The conversation ended with a hug, and the couple continued dancing. Have you ever faced a similar situation—one in which your partner seemed silent and withdrawn, a noticeable departure from his usual demeanor? Or perhaps she is more jovial than is her usual style. Did you wonder what was going on?

In cases such as these, we recommend you use a Couple Talk door opener such as "Is there something up with you?" Delivered with love and concern, this phrase is an invitation to your partner to talk. It's a way of communicating: I care about you and am ready to listen. Go ahead and begin talking. A further communication is: I'm not sure anything is going on with you, but the situation looks and feels different to me. I'm picking up some nonverbal signals that may or may not have meaning. I prefer that we stay conscious about this and talk about it. Are you willing?

Preceding your door-opener phrase with descriptive feedback increases its effectiveness; for example:

"I'm not getting any eye contact from you. [descriptive feedback] Is something up?" [door opener]

"You look distracted. [descriptive feedback] Is there something on your mind?" [door opener]

"The way you've been talking to me tonight feels different than usual. [descriptive feedback] Is something going on that I need to know about?" [door opener]

When approached with a Couple Talk phrase that politely invites a response, most partners will share what is on their minds. But some will not. If your partner denies that an issue exists and needs to be explored, her denial could be accurate or inaccurate. If the denial is accurate, you have incorrectly read the nonverbal signals and no further communication is necessary.

A denial could mean that your partner is not yet in touch with the underlying issue and therefore has nothing to talk about at this time. At this point, she is not aware that her body language and verbal tone are giving off signals. The messages she is communicating nonverbally have not registered in her own consciousness.

Occasionally, a partner will be aware that something is up but doesn't want to talk about it. If that's true, he or she may deny the need to communicate in an effort to wiggle out of the communication process. This is a form of dishonesty and hurts the relationship in the long run.

If you are aware that something is up with you and you don't want to talk about it, say that. An appropriate response might be, "Yes, there is something there. I feel it too. I don't know what it is exactly. I need some time with this one." When you stay conscious and admit to being aware that something new is present, you honor your partner by affirming his or her reality. To distort the truth in this situation is to disrespect your partner by denying their reality. Speak the truth as you know it.

If your partner declines your invitation to talk, don't push it. Pushing and probing have the look and feel of interrogation. No partner enjoys being placed on the witness stand by the other. File your observation away in the back of your mind. Later, if you see additional evidence that confirms your original observation, politely try again to initiate communication. "You sound angry to me. Is there something up with you?"

You cannot make your partner talk if they don't want to. Your best hope to strengthen the lines of communication in these situations is to politely invite them to enter a dialogue with a comment like, "I notice that you're pretty quiet tonight. Is something up?" Then assume the listening stance.

In most cases, as with Sharon and Butch, the ballroom dancers, your invitation will allow you and your partner to resume the dance of emotionally healthy Couple Talk.

If your partner continually refuses to talk, you have new questions to ask—questions addressed to yourself: Why do I continue to stay with someone who won't talk to me? What am I getting out of this? Do I see any sign of this ever changing, and am I willing to live with it if it doesn't change?

HEARING

Hear "Is there something up with you?" as feedback from your partner. He or she is telling you they're picking up signals that all is not well with you. They are reflecting their observations so you can see how you're coming across to them.

"Is there something up with you?" is an invitation to express whatever is on your mind. Your partner is telling you: It's safe for you to talk. If something is bothering you, I'd like to hear about it. I'm ready to listen.

"What is the upside of this?"

"What do you like about it?"

"Tell me the good parts."

"Name some of the benefits."

"Are there positive aspects to this?"

"What was good about your day?"

"Tell me one fun thing that happened."

"WHAT IS THE UPSIDE OF THIS?" is a Couple Talk phrase that can be useful when your partner is caught in a stream of negativity. Use it or one of its variations to break the flow of negative thinking and help him or her create the balance that comes from seeing both sides of a situation.

Nothing is all one way. There is an upside and a downside to everything. There are pluses and minuses, strengths and weaknesses, good points and bad points. "What is the upside?" is a gentle reminder to your partner to look at the other side, to notice the positive aspects of a given situation. Although your husband's job may be stressful or boring, he is employed and bringing home a paycheck. Your wife's parents may be aging, but they are still alive and expressing love and affection. Although your partner is unhappy with his teenager's behavior, at least he and his children are still speaking and working at resolving their issues.

"What is the upside?" is preferable to "Let me tell you the positive side of this." Explaining the benefits, sharing how you see the upside, or detailing the good points of the situation is *telling*. A more effective approach is to provide an opportunity for your partner to discover for themselves the positive side of the situation by asking, "What's good about this?" By personally noticing and articulating the benefits, he or she is more likely to untangle and free themselves from the cycle of negativity.

HEARING

Hear "What is the upside of this?" as a clue that it might be time to examine your line of thinking and talking. Use the question to inquire: Am I only seeing the dark side of this? Am I being overly negative? Do I want to continue to focus on the downside?

"What is the upside of this?" is a gift from your partner. He or she is gifting you with the opportunity to look at your attitude and mood and decide whether it is serving you and your relationship.

"**What was the best part of your day?**"

DO YOU EVER GET TIRED of one-word answers to your questions? Have you had enough of the quick answer that ends the conversation? Perfunctory answers give very little information. They disconnect Couple Talk.

"How was your day today?"

"OK."

"How are you?"

"Fine."

"What's going on?"

"Nothing."

To encourage more than a one-word response, change the flavor of your question. Use Couple Talk that invites a thoughtful response. Ask, "What was the best part of your day?" or a similar question, such as:

"Tell me about something you really liked today."

"What put the biggest smile on your face today?"

"What was the most interesting thing that
happened in your presence today?"

"What did you like best about your birthday?"

"How was this birthday different from all the rest?"

"What surprised you about your trip?"

"What are you looking forward to this weekend?"

"If you could change something that
happened in your day, what would it be
and why would you change it?"

"What happened this time that you'd like
to see happen again?"

These kinds of thought-provoking questions create opportunities for light debriefing. They will help you reconnect with your partner after a day apart from one another. By asking questions of this nature you're communicating the message: I'm interested in you. I want to know more about the details of your day. Help me catch up with what is happening in your life by sharing your thoughts and feelings.

This style of Couple Talk marks the beginning of the process of reflection and indicates a willingness to communicate below the surface level. Add thought-provoking questions to your Couple Talk. You may be surprised and delighted by what you get back.

HEARING

Hearing a question like "What was the best part of your day?" means that your partner is seeking more dialogue. He or she is interested in you, your thoughts, and your feelings. Let yourself feel honored.

You have a partner who desires a deeper understanding of who you are. Strive to provide them with more information, more detail, and specific examples. Allow your words to paint a picture for them. Then ask, "What happened in your day that was similar?"

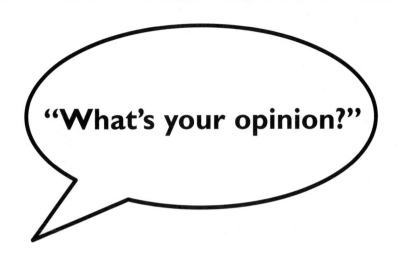

"What's your opinion?"

FOR THE PAST FIVE YEARS Jill had been extremely unhappy with her job. As a legal assistant she wasn't always treated with the respect and consideration she felt she deserved. She had been thinking about quitting and discussed the situation with her husband on several occasions.

One day Jill had enough, crossed the line, and made the decision to quit. That night she told her husband. He became livid and the tone of his response was challenging.

"How could you do such a thing without consulting me?" he demanded.

Jill's counter-response was predictable. "I told you many times I was unhappy and wanted to quit. You never objected and hardly said a thing," she said.

In the months that followed, the quality of Jill's conversations with her husband deteriorated. They became increasingly filled with accusations and mutual distrust. The couple struggled to make decisions and found they were avoiding discussions about jobs, money, and parenting because those conversations often ended in a fight.

Jill and her husband eventually found their way to marital therapy, where they explored several areas of their relationship. One major issue they examined was how communication patterns related to joint decision-making. During the course of their therapy each was challenged to begin using the Couple Talk phrase, "What's your opinion?"

Asking "What's your opinion?" communicates that you want to see the situation through your partner's eyes. You're delivering the message: I'm interested in you. I want to hear your ideas, thoughts, and opinions.

"What's your opinion?" can serve two purposes. One is to elicit information from your partner that will help you arrive at a mutually agreeable decision about an area of concern to you both. The other is to open a dialogue that will help you think through the process of a personal decision and reach your own conclusion.

Some forms of "What's your opinion?" steer the conversation toward a result that requires a direct answer. They include:

"What would you like to do?"

"Where would you like to eat out?"

"What movie would you like to see?"

"What type of vacation would you like to take?"

"Who would you invite to the party?"

Answers to these direct questions are usually short and state a preference.

"I'd like to go for a walk."

"Let's go get pizza."

"I want to vacation by the beach."

Less direct forms of "What's your opinion?" inquire about process.

> "I'm interested in knowing what your opinion is about this."
>
> "I want to know what you're feeling/thinking/wondering."
>
> "I'm looking for another perspective on the matter and I would value your input."

These questions are more open-ended and are an invitation to your partner to explore an issue with you. They indicate that you don't expect them to answer the question for you. You want their help in moving you through the decision-making process. This process of sharing thoughts, feelings, ideas, and concerns creates a deeper level of intimacy, strengthening your bond as a couple. The decisions that result come out wrapped in encouragement, support, and togetherness.

HEARING

When you hear "What's your opinion?" or a similar question, listen carefully. Your partner may be calling upon you for a direct answer to a direct question or they may be inviting you to help them through the process of decision-making. Answer accordingly.

"FRED AND I HAVE MANY MEANINGFUL DISCUSSIONS, BUT FIRST I HAVE TO GET HIS ATTENTION."

"Start anywhere but start talking."

"I don't know how to tell you what I have to say."

"I'm not sure what to say about this."

"I'm not sure I can say this right."

"I don't know if I can have this come out
the way I want to."

"I don't know where to begin."

WHEN YOUR SPOUSE MAKES A STATEMENT like this, lovingly, gently and firmly encourage him or her with the Couple Talk phrase, "Start anywhere, but start talking." Spoken with genuine interest, this phrase invites and encourages your partner to begin the communication process.

Did you ever try to steer a parked car? Impossible, isn't it? Before you can steer a parked car, you have to get the car moving. Once it's moving, steering becomes easy. In fact, once the car is rolling, you can turn it completely around and head it in the opposite direction. The most important part of the process is to get the car moving.

The same holds true for conversation. Get the conversation moving. If your words aren't coming out the way you want them to, you can self-correct as you go. Make adjustments along the way.

The exact order of your comments is not as important as the final destination. Trust the communication process. Trust that the conversation will eventually arrive at the appropriate place. Demonstrate that trust by beginning and continuing the process.

"I'm not sure if I can say this right" and similar expressions are a verbal sign that the speaker may be attempting to control the partner's reaction. Remember, your partner is in charge of his own feelings, interpretations, and reactions. Your job is to say what needs to be said. No cushioning or shock absorbing. Just say what you need to say as clearly, directly, and honestly as possible. If it doesn't come out as accurately as you'd like, change it.

One of the benefits of talking about a concern is that the act of speaking about it helps clarify it in your own mind. Saying it aloud and hearing it as you go will help you become increasingly clear about the issue and thus more able to communicate it accurately to your partner.

HEARING

Hear "Start anywhere, but start talking" as an opportunity to use your partner as a sounding board. Do not hear it as a threat. Do not hear it as probing. What your partner is telling you by her use of this Couple Talk phrase is, Perfection is not required. It's OK to make a mistake in how you say what you want to say. It's OK to struggle for words and concepts of expression. But it is important to begin the dialogue.

"What did I say/do that gave you that idea?"

LATRELL BROWN HAD BEEN DATING Grace for thirteen months. He was surprised when she informed him, "I'm not sure you'd make a good father."

Cassidy Justin had been in a committed relationship for over a year. She was taken aback when her boyfriend mentioned that he thought she was prejudiced.

Robert Arnold was on his fifth date with a young college senior when she suggested they go to a movie instead of a hockey game because she knew he didn't like sports.

Latrell, Cassidy, and Robert were each surprised by their partner's comment. Each chose not to take it personally. Each elected to take a non-defensive stance and responded with a variation of "What did I say that give you that idea?"

In reply to "I'm not sure you'd make a good father," Latrell said, "Help me understand how you came to that conclusion." Cassidy reacted to the comment about prejudice with, "Have you seen some evidence to support that thought?" In an effort to understand the remark about sports, Robert asked, "Will you give me some idea of how I gave that impression?"

Neither Latrell, Cassidy, nor Robert tried to make their partner wrong. Instead, each used the opportunity to increase personal awareness by looking at themselves through their partner's eyes. Each made an effort to learn something about how they were being perceived and how their behavior might have contributed to creating that perception. Each opted to search for understanding rather than become defensive.

"What did I say that gave you that impression?" is Couple Talk that allows for the possibility that there might be some validity to your partner's assertion. It leaves room for the idea that you might be at least partially responsible for their perception. It helps you stay open to the notion that a portion of your partner's interpretation could be true.

"You never pay attention to me."

"You don't value my ideas."

"You don't like my clothes."

"You're afraid to confront me."

"You don't think I know anything about cars."

"You don't like it when I spend time with my family."

"You don't seem to care what I think."

Have you been confronted with assertions similar to these? Did you feel yourself getting defensive? Did you want to give proof that it wasn't so? Instead, why not gather data, do some self-exploration, and move you and your partner closer to mutual understanding with the Couple Talk phrase, "What did I do to give you that idea?"

HEARING

When your partner asks, "What did I do to give you that idea?" hear it as an honest question. Know that he or she probably doesn't agree with your assessment but is open to learning about how they might have created that impression. Give them an honest answer.

"I WANT TO TALK TO YOU. WHICH IS
YOUR IN EAR?"

Ten Things to Do to Help Your Partner Feel Heard

1. Turn off the TV/radio/computer.

2. Look into your partner's eyes.

3. Assume a receptive posture.

4. Sit up in your seat and lean forward.

5. Clarify your partner's point by asking questions.

6. Say less.

7. Schedule a time to talk, and show up.

8. Allow your partner to solve his or her own problem.

9. Empathize with your partner's feelings.

10. Consider your partner's point of view in the matter.

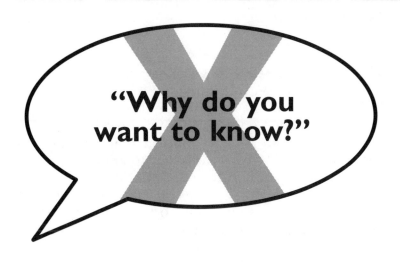

"WHY DO YOU WANT TO KNOW?" is a subtle way of avoiding difficult questions from your partner that require an honest and open reply—questions such as:

"How much did you pay for that?"

"How many sexual partners did you have before me?"

"Why do you always side with your mother?"

"What kinds of things did you do with your previous husband's family?"

"When was your first sexual experience?"

"When was the last time you did something for me?"

"How many times did you do that before you met me?"

"Have you ever lied to me?"

Such questions are an attempt to open communication about something that is troubling your partner.

The "why" response closes it down. Asking "why" is a defensive position that attempts to deflect the heat from oneself and place it back on the other person. It implies: Why do you want to know how many sexual partners I've had? Are you concerned about the number you've had? Why do you want to know if I've lied to you? Have you lied to me? "Why do you want to know?" is a phrase that closes down the lines of communication and is counterproductive to building intimacy and connectedness.

Instead of a "why" response, consider a "what" response. "What is it that you would like to know about my decision to side with my mother?" "What concerns you about my past sexual experiences?" View your partner's question as the first step in a discussion about a topic of concern. Create a dialogue about that concern. For example, you might say, "I'm willing to answer your question and I would like to discuss what concerns you have that prompted the question."

HEARING

When you ask a difficult question of your partner and get the response, "Why do you want to know?" interpret his or her defensiveness as a request for help. Being angry or defensive in return will not help the situation. Restate your question in a less direct way or withdraw it. Say, "You seem bothered by my question. Let's talk about my concerns at another time," or "Let me rephrase my question in a way that addresses my concern in a better way."

TIMES TO REMAIN SILENT

1. When your partner is deep in reflection.

2. When you and your partner are taking in the beauty of nature: watching the sun set, gazing into a waterfall, viewing a rainbow.

3. When you're walking in the woods, holding hands.

4. When you're watching your child engrossed in play.

5. At moments of high stress.

6. When your partner is venting.

7. When you're so angry you feel you could burst.

8. When it looks like your partner could explode with anger.

9. When your partner is trying to make a point.

10. When it's your turn to listen.

11. When you're attempting to understand.

12. When it's already quiet. Let your mind enjoy the calm.

CHAPTER 2

The Language of Feelings

"I hurt when you
say those things
to me."

COMMUNICATION OF FEELINGS is a basic skill in the
Couple Talk system. "I hurt when you say those things
to me" and similar phrases will help you learn and
master this important communication technique.

While you are first learning to express feelings we
recommend you focus on the four basic feelings:
anger, pain (hurt), pleasure, and fear. You may have
heard them referred to as mad, sad, glad, and scared.
All other feelings or emotions are a combination of
one or two of these four feelings. The four basic feelings could be stated as:

"I hurt when you say those things to me."

"I'm angry when you say those things to me."

"I'm sad when you say those things to me."

"I'm happy when you say those things to me."

An essential ingredient when communicating feelings is to structure your language in a way that owns
your feeling. Take responsibility for your feeling by
beginning your expression of it with an "I" state-

ment. "I hurt," "I am angry," "I am sad," and "I feel happy" are examples of a self-responsible expression of feelings.

When you report your feelings to your partner with a "YOU" statement, you disown responsibility for them. "*You* make me angry," "*You* are depressing me," and "*You* make me happy" are examples of giving your partner responsibility for your feelings. (For more information on language that disowns responsibility see the Couple Talk phrase "*You make me mad*" later in this chapter.)

By saying, "I hurt when you say those things to me," you own your feeling as well as validate it. Your language does not blame your partner for how you feel. It provides them with information about how you feel when they manifest a specific behavior. It gives them feedback about the types of situations in which you feel hurt, angry, sad, or happy.

"I hurt when you say those things to me" and similar Couple Talk phrases have three parts. The first part requires that you identify your feelings and put them into words. This can be difficult if you are not used to expressing feelings—if you have not been raised by parents who effectively modeled the skill or if your belief system tells you feelings are better left unacknowledged. If that is the case for you, begin by focusing on the four basic feelings. Ask yourself: Am I feeling sadness, anger, joy, or fear? Identify one of the basic feelings and express it as simply as possible. "I feel angry" is sufficient. So is "I hurt."

The second part of this Couple Talk phrase deals with "when."

"I feel angry when . . ."

"I hurt when . . ."

"I get sad when . . ."

As you structure and communicate the "when" part, be specific. Offer pertinent information that will help your partner understand why you are feeling the way you do. Be descriptive, painting a picture with your words. The more specific you can be, the better your chance of communicating clearly what you feel.

Avoid broad references and inferences. Instead of saying, "I hurt when you don't pay attention to me," say, "I hurt when you spend more time with your buddies on the softball team than you do with me." To give your partner a more accurate view of your present state, change "I'm angry when you discount me" to "I'm angry when you ask me what I want to do and then you do what you want anyway."

To help your partner better understand his role in how you feel say, "I hurt when you say that I'm lazy," "I'm scared when you yell and call me a bitch," or "I'm sad when you hear I was in a car accident and appear more worried about the car than you are about what happened to me."

To further clarify your feelings and your partner's role in them we recommend a third step—the addition of a "because" statement.

"I'm angry when you don't turn off the TV when we talk to one another because it seems like you don't consider my words important."

"I hurt when you stare at other women when you're with me in public because it seems as if you would rather be with them than with me."

"I'm filled with joy when I see you play with the children like that because it reminds me of the times we played together as a young couple."

"I'm scared when you use that tone of voice with me because it seems threatening and overpowering."

Adding a "because" statement is a good way to stay clear about why you're feeling the way you are. It will help to explain and support the "when" part of the statement. Think of the "because" part as the equivalent of using training wheels to learn to ride a bicycle. In time, as you and your partner become more accustomed to expressing feelings and responding to one another, you can drop the training wheels and eliminate the "because" portion of this technique.

HEARING

Hearing your partner express feelings requires the ability to allow him or her to feel however they choose. Be mindful of your own feelings here. It is not necessary to adjust your feelings to match your partner's. If she is angry, you don't have to be angry also. If he hurts, you don't have to hurt more. If she is sad, you don't have to rescue her by trying to cheer her up.

As the receiver of this Couple Talk phrase, you are being challenged to explore your role in how your partner feels. Resist letting yourself feel threatened by his expression of feelings. Welcome it as an opportunity to understand and grow closer. Remain open to the possibility that you may be contributing to her emotional state in some way. See what is here for you to learn. Be willing to discover. Be willing to listen. Be willing to simply be present.

"I'm feeling frustrated."

Maryanne was raised by parents who did not regularly share feelings. She had no role models for how to do that effectively. As a result, by the time she married, her "feeling vocabulary" was severely limited.

In addition, Maryanne believed that if she told her husband her negative feelings, he would stop loving her. She thought that sharing them would seriously damage the relationship and that she would appear to her husband to be a weak person who could not manage her feelings effectively. Consequently, she habitually choked them off, numbed them out, and kept them to herself.

When Maryanne did share her feelings, she communicated them in an unskillful fashion. She shared them the way many people do, by focusing on what the other person is doing wrong. "You're always late and that frustrates me," she would say. "You drive so fast. It's so annoying," she once told her husband.

Because her skill level was low, the reaction she got whenever she did share her feelings didn't encourage her to continue the practice. Each time she expressed a feeling she reconfirmed her belief that she would get less love and do damage to the relationship by making those feelings known.

In counseling, Maryanne learned to express her feelings clearly and cleanly. She learned to recognize them, state them simply, and communicate what she thought was contributing to their arising. She also learned that she didn't have to use her husband's behavior to justify them.

Over time, Maryanne became skilled at stating what she was feeling cleanly and tying it to a reason. Instead of "You drive so fast. It's so annoying," she might say, "When you drive fast I get frightened." She learned to replace the finger-pointing in statements like, "You're always late and it frustrates me," with "I'm feeling frustrated about not being there on time."

When Maryanne's husband forgot their anniversary, she felt hurt. She wanted to tell him about her pain but she wanted to do it effectively. She knew she would add gasoline to the fire if she used Couple Talk such as, "You're going to ruin this relationship if you keep doing this," or "You're a rotten husband." So she continued to explore possibilities. She considered more tactful responses, like, "Why did you forget our anniversary?" or "It's tough living with you sometimes," but rejected them because they sounded accusatory or vague to her.

The statement Maryanne eventually chose to share with her husband was, "When you don't acknowledge our anniversary, I get scared that you might be growing away from me. And I hurt."

By owning her feelings and by stating her thoughts clearly and simply without an accusatory tone, Maryanne invited her spouse to enter a dialogue concerning this important situation. Her husband heard her feelings and was able to respond to them empathetically. He did not feel compelled to use words to defend himself or offer counter-accusations. Intimacy was served and the end result was an increase in the couple's feelings of love and affection for one another.

HEARING

When your partner shares a feeling with an "I" statement—"I feel angry"—and offers further information as explanation, resist the urge to become defensive. Hear the feeling as a statement about her, not as a statement about you. She is not talking about you. She is talking about herself. Focus on understanding rather than defending or explaining.

If your spouse shares feelings unskillfully, disowning responsibility for them while making you wrong for something you did or said, it is still possible to *hear* the verbalization as if she had expressed it skillfully. If she says, "You hurt me when you flirt with other women," hear, I'm scared that you don't find me attractive anymore, and when I see you talking to other women I'm reminded of that fear. Respond not to what she said, but rather to what she would have said if she had taken the time to think about and construct a skillful sharing of her feelings.

If she tells you, "How could you let your mother talk to me like that? You tick me off!" hear the message as if she had delivered it skillfully: I'm angry. I don't like it when your mother attacks my parenting style and I would like it if you would help me defend myself.

Remember, *she* is in charge of how she says it. *You* are in charge of how you hear it.

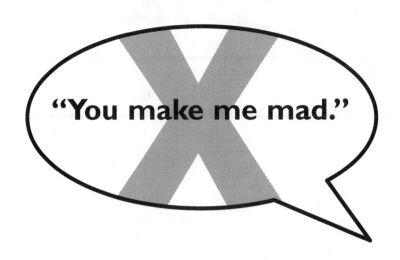

"You're beginning to irritate me."

"That makes me happy."

"You're making me nervous."

"You're depressing me."

"You always drag me down."

"You're gladdening my heart."

"You're frustrating me."

"You're rubbing me the wrong way."

THESE ARE EXAMPLES of Couple Talk language that disowns responsibility for your own feelings and actions. They assign responsibility to your partner and diminish your sense of personal power.

"You make me mad" is a way of speaking and thinking that gives your partner credit for your anger. "You're depressing me" assigns him responsibility for your depression. "That makes me so happy" credits her for the joy you're feeling. When members of a couple speak and think in ways that give their partner control over their happiness, they tend to believe they can only be happy if their partner behaves in a certain way. Their degree of happiness is then at the mercy of their partner's actions and moods. There is no personal power in that style of thinking.

Actually, no one can *make* you happy. No one can make you mad, either. In fact, no one can make you feel anything. It is simply not possible for another person to create an emotion in you. Emotions are your personal response to an outside event and are within your power to control. Maybe your partner is purposefully trying to make you mad. You don't have to bite the hook. Your emotional reactions and physical actions are still under your control. They remain your responsibility.

When you begin to think and believe that your spouse can "make" you mad, the reverse also seems true. You begin to buy in to the false notion that you can make him or her mad as well. If you are responsible for your partner's anger, then you have to walk around on egg shells, being careful not to do anything that will "make" them mad.

There is a name for believing you make your spouse happy, mad, sad, or depressed and that it's your job to control his or her emotions. It's called codependence. When you believe and talk as if you are in charge of another's feelings, you blur the boundaries between two distinct individuals and begin to give your Self away. It takes clear boundaries between two people to make a relationship work without codependence. Using "makes me" Couple Talk does nothing to create clear definitions of where one person ends and another begins.

We are not saying don't have feelings. Feelings are important and need to be expressed on a regular basis. What we are saying is take ownership for your feelings by using self-responsible language.

"I feel hurt" is more accurate than "You're hurting me."

"I'm choosing to be irritated about this" lets you retain more personal power than "You're irritating me to no end."

"I'm doing frustration right now" puts you in a better position to control your own frustration than "You're frustrating the heck out of me."

"I'm experiencing this as scary" reflects more ownership of your feeling than "You scare me when you do that."

Irritation, depression, anxiety, joy, and other emotional reactions are not something that your partner causes in you. They are not created by the event or the person initiating the event. They are created by how your mind interprets the event, by the thoughts you think, by the beliefs you activate or the images you create in your head.

Use Couple Talk that owns your feelings.

"I'm angry."

"I'm frustrated."

"I'm thrilled."

Speak in a way that takes responsibility for your emotional reactions to the events of your life.

"I'm doing anxiety about this situation."

"I'm creating frustration."

"My thoughts are producing joy."

Create clear boundaries between your partner's actions and your feeling responses.

"I'm choosing to be filled with joy right now."

"Depression is the feeling that I'm producing."

We're wondering how you're reacting to the "makes me" information presented here. Pay attention to the words you use as you think about it. Is the information "making you" excited, or are you choosing to see it as helpful? Is it depressing you, or are you choosing to be depressed by it? Is it thrilling you, or are you creating extreme joy with it?

Whatever your reaction to this material, be sure to own it by using self-responsible language.

HEARING

If your partner says, "You make me mad," or "You're upsetting me," know that he or she is in the midst of strong feeling. Refrain from giving them a language lesson by explaining to them that they are creating their own feeling. Focus on the feeling itself rather than argue about who or what is responsible for it. Use the listening skills described in the previous chapter and elsewhere in this book to acknowledge the feeling your partner is experiencing and to help them feel heard.

**"I FEEL ANGRY WHEN YOU DON'T
RESPOND TO MY QUESTIONS."**

"Ouch! That sounds like a put-down."

WOMEN DON'T wake up in the morning saying to themselves, Today I'm going to tear into my partner, deliver several put-downs that will eat away at his self-esteem, degrade his interpersonal skills, and question his manhood. Men don't intentionally come up with five or six negative comments, add them to a put-down list, and distribute them intermittently to their partner throughout the day. Yet, to watch the way some partnerships operate, it seems that this is the case.

Partners who put each other down don't always send those put-downs consciously. At times, people are simply unaware that their words mock, belittle, or tease. They do not realize that the words they just spoke can be hurtful because they are heard as a put-down.

What is needed is a Couple Talk phrase that will give the speaker feedback about how his or her message was received—let them "hear" themselves as they sound to their partner—and simultaneously communicate the recipient's feelings. "Ouch! That sounds like a put-down" fits the bill. "Ouch" lets your partner know there was a sting associated with their words. "That sounds like a put-down" clears up any misconceptions about how the message was interpreted.

Use "Ouch! That sounds like a put-down" in response to any of these thinly-veiled put-downs.

"Are you going to wear that?"

"You're not going to tell that story again, are you?"

"Have you seen yourself in the mirror lately?"

"Are you going to eat that whole bag?"

"You might want to consider retaking driver's training."

"Bad hair day?"

"You been on the scale lately?"

"Forget your brains?"

"What's the matter with you?"

"Forget how to walk?"

"Failed again, eh?"

"You're worse than the kids."

"Maybe you'll get it right this time."

"Mr. Sensitive today, eh?"

"Blue is not your best color."

"Having a 'senior moment'?"

"Do I have to explain it again?"

"You have no sense of humor."

"I might as well be talking to the dog."

"That's a bit presumptuous, isn't it?"

"The way you think scares me sometimes."

"That's silly."

HEARING

When your partner says, "Ouch! That feels like a put-down," pay attention. There is an important message in those words. It doesn't matter whether or not your comment was intended as a put-down. It was received as one. Respond with that in mind.

Resist the urge to defend yourself. Use this feedback to self-confront. Did you intentionally put your partner down? If so, is there a more effective way you could share your anger or frustration? If you did not intend a put-down, was there something about your tone or choice of words that may have given that impression? Could you rephrase your concern to increase the chance that it will be received the way you intend it?

"Please talk to me like I'm someone you love."

BOB AND JAN were out on their sailboat for an afternoon of pleasure. A soft and steady breeze provided a perfect day for smooth sailing in the warm summer sun. As the wind pushed the boat along, Bob interrupted the calm by yelling, "Jan, are you blind? Can't you see you're off line?"

"I'm trying to get back on course," Jan replied.

"Give me the damn wheel," Bob commanded, as he stepped in and took over.

Hurt and saddened by the brief exchange, Jan disappeared below.

Later, after Jan returned topside, Bob inquired about her quiet disposition. "What's your problem now?" he asked.

"I'm hurt by the way you spoke to me earlier," Jan informed him.

"Can't you take a little criticism?" Bob asked.

"I'm willing to take criticism and even hear your anger. I can handle that. But when you do it, I'd like you to talk to me like I'm someone you love."

"What does this have to do with love?" Bob wondered aloud.

"I don't feel love right now," Jan replied softly. "And I don't feel love when you talk to me like you did when I was off course."

After a moment of silence Bob asked, "So how should I talk to you about my concerns when we're on the boat?" The respectful conversation that followed restored the pleasant atmosphere and brought love back into the present moment. The day's adventure was salvaged and the relationship moved forward, with each partner taking another step toward intimacy, connectedness, and each other.

"Please talk to me like I'm someone you love" is Couple Talk that will help you and your partner focus on the HOW of communication. In any verbal exchange, how you say what you say is just as important as the content of your communication. Whether you're talking about finances, parenting, sex, in-laws, household responsibilities, or the steering of a boat, how you say what you say is critical to your partner's perception of your message. "Please talk to me like I'm someone you love" is Couple Talk that can serve as a reminder to you and your partner that one important goal of your relationship is to stay connected as you move through the communication process. A variation could be offered in the middle of an argument. "Hold up. Let's stop a second. I want to continue to talk about this, but let's do it while we both remember the person we're talking to is someone we love." Or at the beginning of a discussion you might say, "This has the potential to be a heated discussion. Let's keep in mind that we're each talking to someone we love."

"Please talk to me like I'm someone you love" is a reminder that the love you have for one another needs to be honored, even when you disagree or argue. In order to do that, be mindful of your tone of voice, facial expression, and body posture. Soften your voice, drop the accusatory tone, and alter your defensive stance. Wrap your words in love. Say whatever it is you want to say in a way that shows genuine concern for the person to whom you're saying it.

If your partner refuses or is unable to talk to you like you're someone he or she loves, it is possible to change how you hear them. They may not be skilled at communicating in loving tones. You can listen in love anyway. You can choose to focus on the content of the message rather than on the style of delivery. Although you're not being talked to like someone who is loved, you can choose to listen like someone who loves by refusing to hear accusation. Listen actively rather than defensively. Listen with a mood of forgiveness, remembering that your partner lacks skill and not love. Hear the content the way you wish it was sent rather than focusing on the unskillful process by which it was delivered. Say to yourself, I'm going to listen to him/her like he/she is someone I love.

HEARING

If you hear your partner say, "Please talk to me like I'm someone you love," you can be sure your communication style has ruffled some feathers. What he or she is telling you is: I'm not feeling loved right now. I'm pretty sure you love me, but it isn't coming across in the way you're talking to me. I don't want you to change the content of your message, but would you take a serious look at how you're delivering it? Hear it as an opportunity to say what you want to say in a way that communicates love as well as content.

THINK ABOUT THE LAST TIME you heard your partner say, "I'm fine," in response to a question about how he or she was feeling. Or perhaps they uttered a similar phrase, like "I'm okay," "Everything's all right," "Can't complain," or "It could be worse." Those short responses don't give you much information, do they?

"I'm fine" and other quick answers are common responses that people use when they don't want to give much thought to your question. They serve to keep the conversation at a surface level or, at worst, become an avoidance tactic to employ when they don't want to talk about feelings. These short responses are indirect ways of saying, I don't want to address the issue right now. The person's hope is that if they provide a brief response they will be left alone and not pushed for additional information.

You've no doubt experienced situations where you've suspected something is up with your partner—situations where he or she is unusually quiet, you can almost see smoke streaming from their ears, and you can hear their heart pounding from across the room. Although all the nonverbal signals suggest otherwise, when you inquire into their condition they respond, "I'm fine."

We recommend you only use "I'm fine!" when you really *are* fine. Come to an agreement with your partner that you will use this phrase only when you are truly fine. Agree to say what you mean and mean what you say.

If you're not fine, it serves no one to respond to your partner's inquiry about your emotional state with, "I'm fine." Instead, we recommend a more direct approach. Be honest. If you don't want to talk, say, "I don't want to talk about this right now." If your desire is for space and privacy and you're feeling pressured by your partner's questions, respond with "I'll let you know when I'm ready to talk about it."

HEARING

When your partner says, "I'm fine!" and you sense that something else is going on, hear a request for space. Consider that he or she might not be skilled at asking for the space they need. They may be struggling with the feelings they are having and need time to sort them out. Instead of becoming accusatory and making a comment like, "Well, you don't look fine to me," invite discussion with Couple Talk that honors your partner's hidden request. Ask, "Is there something up with you?" (see Chapter 1) or say, "It seems to me . . ." (see Chapter 5).

If your partner is still hesitant, avoid pressing for more information and return to the issue later. Say, "Let me know when you're ready to tell me" (see Chapter 8). The following day you can say, "Yesterday you seemed angry [or hurt, or sad] about something. Would you like to talk about it?"

Describe, Describe, Describe

BONITA'S HUSBAND NOTICED his brand-new toolbox sitting outside on the porch. As he watched the rain pour down on it, he wanted to give his wife one of his eloquent lectures on respect for materials. Instead, he said, "Bonita, I see my new tool box getting soaked in the rain. I'm angry. Tools need to be returned to the garage when you're finished with them."

Chad's partner felt irritation when he saw dirty dishes in the den. He was tempted to vent his frustration with words that shame. He resisted his urge to scold and said instead, "Chad, there are dirty dishes in the den. I feel irritated. Dirty dishes need to be rinsed and placed in the dishwasher."

Bonita's husband and Chad's partner were each successful in getting the behavior they wanted. Each used a valuable Couple Talk strategy: the Describe, Describe, Describe technique. In the midst of strong emotion, they described what they saw. They described what they felt. And they described what needed to be done.

By focusing your Couple Talk on descriptions, you keep from attacking character and personality. You refrain from wounding the spirit. By using the Describe, Describe, Describe technique you speak to the situation rather than to the character of your partner. "I see wet towels on the bathroom floor" describes the situation. This style of speaking is preferable to "Why can't you remember to pick up your towels?" which attacks your partner's character. "I see my new tool box getting soaked in the rain" speaks to the situation at hand, while "Can't you be more respectful of my tools?" points to your partner's personality.

"I'm feeling frustrated" or "I'm angry" describes how you are feeling. You get to be angry. You get to be irritated. You get to be annoyed. And you certainly get to express those feelings. The goal is to send a clear message that communicates your feelings without wounding the spirit or attacking the character of your partner. That is done best by wrapping your feelings in descriptive language rather than accusatory language. To do this effectively, identify your feeling and express it directly.

Direct communication of feelings is done with "I" statements. "I" statements begin with "I" and show ownership for the feeling: "I'm angry." "I'm feeling annoyed." "I'm experiencing sadness." If you begin your sentence with "you," as in "*You* are making me angry" and "*You* are frustrating me," you are not owning your feeling or expressing it cleanly.

"Towels belong on the hangers behind the bathroom door" describes what needs to be done. So does "Tools need to be returned to the garage when you're finished with them." When your language focuses on what needs to be done, you are speaking to the situation. Your language points to the solution rather than to the person who created the problem.

Expressing irritation, frustration, anger, and similar emotions is not only allowed, it is appropriate and necessary. However, expression of feelings needs to be done effectively. When tempted to belittle, scold, lecture, or attack, remember to Describe, Describe, Describe. Describe what you see or hear. "I see that the gas tank is near empty." Describe your feelings. "I feel irritated." Describe what needs to be done. "My car needs to be returned with enough gas for me to get to work."

The Describe, Describe, Describe technique is no guarantee that your partner's behavior will match your desires. It is certain, though, that your words will refrain from attacking character or personality. Your language will show the respect you hope to elicit from your partner. And it will mean that you are becoming increasingly skilled at using nonjudgmental, healthy Couple Talk.

HEARING

If you recognize that your partner is using the Describe, Describe, Describe technique, know that he or she is working hard to express their feelings in healthy ways. Listen to the feeling. Listen to the behavior your partner is describing. Listen to the solution they're suggesting. Honor their efforts to send clear feeling messages by taking them seriously and not personally. They are not talking about your character. They are not name-calling or ridiculing your personality. Your partner is speaking about him- or herself, telling you what they find irritating, annoying, or saddening. Give them credit for being committed to your relationship and to developing the communication skills recommended in this book.

CHAPTER 3

The Language of Intimacy

"I noticed you did the dishes."

"I noticed that you've have been using
some Couple Talk phrases."

"I see that you've been wearing those
shirts I bought for you."

"I noticed you seem really tired
when you get home."

"I NOTICED" is a five-second shot of self-esteem. It says to your partner, I see you. You will not be invisible here.

Everyone likes to be noticed. You like to be noticed. Your partner likes to be noticed. That's one reason why the two of us write books and give seminars. We enjoy the attention that goes with the territory.

I don't need to be noticed, you may be thinking. If so, pay attention to your reaction the next time you enter the room and your partner continues to read the paper without even looking up at you. Think about how you feel when you suggest an idea at a committee meeting and no one responds to it. If you're like most people, you begin to feel invisible, unimportant, undervalued.

To notice your partner is to affirm his or her existence and importance in your life. It acknowledges their presence and communicates that they are valued and appreciated.

When you use this Couple Talk phrase, descriptions are preferable to evaluations. The goal of using "I noticed" is simply to communicate to your partner that you notice them, not to evaluate, rate, or judge them.

Refrain from using Couple Talk that includes an appraisal of your partner's effort, energy, product, or behavior. The following statements are examples of evaluative "I notice" comments.

"I see you did a good job mowing the grass."

"I noticed you did a nice job folding the laundry."

"I watched you play with the children.
You were excellent."

Examples of descriptive statements that communicate you have noticed your partner's behavior without evaluating it include:

"I notice you're almost finished with that book."

"I saw that you filled my car with gas."

"I notice you've been getting up in time to
enjoy an extra cup of coffee."

Add "I noticed" to your Couple Talk and to your self-talk. Tell yourself, I notice that I've been implementing Couple Talk phrases on a consistent basis, or I notice the positive effect these phrases are having on my attitude. If you haven't noticed your implementation efforts, why not begin now, with the phrase, "I noticed . . ."?

HEARING

If you notice "I notice" coming from your partner, tell them that you noticed their noticing. Laugh about how each of you is "techniquing" the other and enjoying it. Be assured that the feeling of using a technique will fall away as you become skillful at using this kind of Couple Talk and integrate the strategy into your normal style of communicating.

Hear "I noticed" as an effort by your partner to tell you that you're important to them—to let you know that you're valued. Enjoy the attention. You deserve it.

"Let's explore this together."

"Dream with me for a moment."

"Join me in this dance."

"Can we do this together?"

"Let's make this a joint adventure."

"Let's see if we can stumble across
something new today."

"I'm willing to make a mistake. Want to
make one with me?"

"Let's unravel this mystery together."

THE INTENT of "Come journey with me" is that of
invitation. This Couple Talk phrase and others like it,
such as those above, is a summons to your partner to
join with you in adventure, discovery, and change. It's
an invitation to create a new journey, together.

Often when you use this phrase, the destination is
unclear. The outcome is unknown. The steps are not
listed. There is no timeline. What is clear is that you

and your partner are agreeing to go through the process together.

The desire to invite your partner to journey with you may arise on numerous occasions throughout your life. This form of Couple Talk could be used in the face of illness or death. "I've just been diagnosed with breast cancer. Will you stay close to me during this difficult time?" It would be appropriate at a time of searching and growth. "I'm not happy with my job and I want to go back to school to change careers. Can you support me in this?" The invitation could be issued in a time of fear. "I'm really not ready to have children right now and I know you are. How might we continue to move forward in our relationship at this time?" It could express a sense of adventure. "I'd like to try some new sexual positions. Let's explore this together." It could be used in a time of uncertainty. "I'm not sure how I feel about our relationship. Will you go to a marriage therapist with me?"

When you use Couple Talk to invite your partner to journey with you, you are really saying, No matter what I'm going through right now, I want to go through it with you. You are asking your partner for their support, encouragement, energy, companionship, and love as you enter unknown territory.

The steps you take on this journey may change all the steps that follow. Wouldn't you like to take those steps with your partner? Ask him or her to join you in this exploration of unknown territory. Turn your journey into a relationship-strengthening event. Seek, find, uncover, discover, scavenge, encounter, unearth, redo, stumble, overtake, pinpoint, unravel, rescue, envision, dream, learn, grow. And do it together.

It is possible that your invitation could produce a negative response. Your partner may say, "No, I can't support you in that," or "I don't want to go talk to a therapist." Their response could be, "No, I'm not comfortable with trying a new sexual position," or "I'm not willing to make that kind of mistake with you." If the answer to the invitation to join you is no, then your present situation calls for a different Couple Talk strategy. It's time to ask a WHAT question.

The WHAT question technique will help you and your partner get clear on "what" they are able to do, "what" they are unwilling to do, and "what" is preventing them from stretching their limit in this situation. Helpful questions are:

"What worries you about going to a
therapist with me?"

"What are some of the concerns you have
about supporting me in this?"

"What bothers you about trying a new
sexual position with me?"

This type of question, delivered with an open heart, will help you remain receptive to your partner's feelings and concerns, maintain the connection between you, and give both of you useful information with which to further the discussion. It may well become the first step in creating a new journey together.

HEARING

Hear this offer as an invitation. It is not a demand. There is no obligation involved. There is no right or wrong answer to the request. What is wanted is an answer that reflects whatever seems real and right for you.

When you are invited to "Come and journey with me," remember that whatever it is your partner wants to do, he or she wants to do it together with you.

Take a moment before answering. Get in touch with your thoughts and your feelings. Ask yourself, Can I truly do what my partner is inviting me to do? Can I really support them in this? Does it feel right for me? Answer honestly. Tell your partner what you are thinking and how you are feeling. If you have mixed feelings, let them know. Stay connected as you address any concerns that arise.

"Come closer."

NADINE AND SYED entered couple counseling because of a recurrent struggle in their relationship. Nadine would come home after a long day at work and an hour commute wanting to move slowly, get out of her work clothes, and sit quietly for an hour. Syed, who had been home by himself for over an hour, was ready to talk about the day and plan an evening together. He had been waiting for Nadine and was eager to connect.

Nadine felt smothered by Syed's immediate attention and would ask him for some space. She found herself using language like, "Please leave me alone," "I need some alone time," and "Please back off!"

Syed felt rejected and isolated.

In a joint counseling session, Syed revealed his confusion. "I get so many 'leave me alone' and 'back off' messages that I think Nadine doesn't like being with me. I don't know what she wants anymore."

"I like being with you lots of times," his wife responded. "I enjoy your company and I do want to be with you."

"It sure doesn't feel like it," Syed told her.

At this point the therapist interrupted their dialogue. "Nadine, you're pretty clear with Syed when you need some space," she said. "How could you let him know those times when you enjoy being around him?"

"I suppose I could tell him," Nadine replied.

"And what would that sound like?"

"Come here and spend some time with me," she suggested.

Syed smiled. "Boy, would I like to hear that," he said.

Over time, Nadine learned to verbalize her desire when she wanted to be close to Syed. She learned and used many variations of the "Come closer" message, including:

"Sit next to me."

"Can I have a hug?"

"Touch me."

"Let's have sex."

"Let's snuggle."

"Talk to me."

"Be with me."

"I want some of you."

"Let's go on a date."

With just this slight adjustment in their Couple Talk, Nadine and Syed quickly began to reconnect.

The adjustment for Nadine was one of balance. She had neglected to balance the Couple Talk phrase "Back off" (see Chapter 7, "The Language of Boundaries") with its antithesis, "Come closer." The two phrases work in tandem. The more you use "Back off," the more you need to use, "Come closer." The more you express "Come closer," the easier it will be to communicate "Back off" when it is appropriate. Each phrase requires the balance provided by the other.

"Come closer" is the message that needs to be used first. When your partner regularly hears "Come closer" and feels the genuine desire it represents, he or she will be better able to honor your request for time and space since they now know that it will likely be balanced with closeness and togetherness in the future.

HEARING

When you hear "Come closer," your partner is calling for connection. He or she is calling you to them. They want to be near you, physically and emotionally. Feel their desire to have you as a part of their life. Hear the attempt to balance "Back off" with closeness. Give their request for closeness the same respect you would give their request for space.

"I want some time
with you."

WHEN HER CHILDREN WERE YOUNG, "I want Mama!"
was a phrase Sheri heard frequently. When one of her
youngsters fell down and skinned a knee, "I want
Mama" were the words used to summon nurturing. "I
want Mama" became a call for help, a plea for attention, and a request for problem-solving.

The use of the "I want Mama" mantra diminished
over the years as Sheri's children grew in age and
independence. By the time they went off to college,
she hadn't heard that phrase in years.

With the kids grown and gone, Sheri became more
focused on her accounting firm, devoting the majori-
ty of her time to it. She often brought work home to
complete after dinner and on weekends. In the middle
of preparing a report one evening she was surprised
when her husband, Barry, tapped her on the shoulder,
looked her in the eye, and said, "I want Mama!" Sheri
couldn't help but smile. She knew exactly what he
meant. In his own sweet way, Barry was saying, "I want
some time with you."

The Couple Talk phrase "I want some time with
you" is a way of saying, I miss you, I want to connect

with you, I want to feel your touch, I want to look into your eyes. When you use this phrase you are asking your partner, Please create space for quality time with me.

Couples often engage in parallel interaction where they sit in the same room, often side by side, traveling down separate tracks, doing separate things. It looks like they're together but they're not. They may even be sitting right next to each other, but one is reading the newspaper and the other is watching TV. He might be engrossed with the computer while she is reading a current best seller. Or perhaps she's working on the budget while he dries the dishes. Often, couples give the appearance of being together, yet they aren't connecting.

There is nothing wrong with being engaged in parallel activities. Doing separate things in close proximity to one's partner is a necessary part of living together. The strategy helps couples to get things done and allows for different interests while still being together.

The purpose of "I want some time with you" is to send a message to your partner about the *quality* of time being shared. Quantity is not the issue here. "I want some time with you" is a request to intersect emotionally, spiritually, mentally, or physically. It is a call to move from parallel togetherness to a more intimate form of connectedness.

Other phrases that communicate a desire for closeness include:

"How about some QT [quality time]?"

"Let's reconnect."

"I'd like to focus."

"Let's be on the same track for a while."

Create your own special "I want some time" phrase with your partner. It could be one whose meaning only the two of you know. You could borrow a phrase from another generation, as Barry did with "I want Mama." Or you may choose to simply use the signature phrase for this section, "I want some time with you." Regardless of which words you use, remember that it's always OK to ask for some "mama time."

HEARING

The use of the Couple Talk phrase "I want some time with you" is a call for love and connection. It doesn't mean, Let's go in the other room and watch TV. It is not a request to engage in a different parallel activity in which you remain alone together. It is a request to intersect in a meaningful way. Hear this communication as, I need eye contact, touch, softness, interaction with you. It is a plea for quality time. Take the request seriously.

"CERTAINLY YOU MAY TALK TO ME A FEW MINUTES, BUT NOT PRIME TIME MINUTES."

"Would you do me a favor?"

JACK DIDN'T LIKE TO ASK his wife Maxine for help. He preferred to do things for himself. He was good at "doing." He was a goal-oriented, active achiever. He got things done, on time. His efforts produced quality work.

There was only one problem. Maxine felt left out. She was unable to contribute to her husband's accomplishments. Because she rarely got to help, Maxine experienced a void in her life. That void eventually produced distance in the relationship. When Jack noticed the distance and Maxine articulated how she felt, the couple sought help from a professional counselor.

In therapy, Jack learned to "gift" his wife with his receiving. He realized that although he repeatedly gave, he was neither skilled at nor comfortable with being on the receiving end. Since he had always gained self-esteem and approval from accomplishing things, he found it difficult at first to believe his wife would like him better if she were needed.

Slowly, over time, Jack came to realize that the relationship was strengthened when giving and receiving became a two-way street. Although he still works on some projects alone, he is now able to both give and receive and finds personal satisfaction in each. Maxine values helping and no longer feels left out.

Like Maxine, many people want to be needed. They are willing to do for others. Yet they aren't always sure exactly what to do or what is appropriate. That's where "Will you do me a favor?" comes in. When you ask your partner, "Will you do me a favor?" you give direction to his or her desire to be of service, to demonstrate love, to help out.

You are not being an imposition when you ask for help. On the contrary, you are giving your partner a gift. You are gifting her with an opportunity to contribute, to feel valuable, to return the help that you have given in the past.

Keep in mind that when you ask for a favor you just might be doing your partner a favor.

HEARING

When your partner asks for a favor, he or she wants help. They are inviting you to contribute to their well-being. They are giving you an opportunity to share your love. Decide if doing the favor is a price you can pay. If it isn't, say so and tell them why. If it is, make a gift of your giving and let your partner enjoy the receiving.

"Would you like
a back rub?"

"WOULD YOU LIKE A BACK RUB?" is an offer to give
your partner pleasure. It flows from two important
and related beliefs. One belief is that giving pleasure
to another builds intimacy. Connectedness and feelings of closeness grow as one person provides pleasure
to the other. The second belief is that giving and
receiving are two sides of the same coin. As we give
pleasure, we get pleasure in return—the pleasure of
giving, the pleasure of pleasing, the pleasure of seeing
the beloved enjoying the receiving.

This type of pleasuring carries no demands. An
hour or two of massage and sensual touch is not
intended to lead to sexual intercourse. It is important
to have no hidden expectations or agenda. The motivation is simply to have your partner feel good.

"How about a face massage?"

"May I rub your sore muscle?"

"If your feet are sore, put them up here in
my lap. I'll help them feel better."

These forms of physical pleasuring can be planned or occur spontaneously. They can evolve into a Friday night ritual or be an occasional break from routine. They can take two hours or two minutes.

Whatever form they take, concentrate on giving as much pleasure as you can. You are helping your partner relax. You are helping them trust. You are helping them enjoy receiving. You are helping them enjoy their body.

Also, tune in to your own pleasure. Enjoy the pleasure that comes from pleasing your partner. You both deserve it.

HEARING

Hear "Would you like a back rub?" as an offer to receive pleasure. Your partner is reaching out to you in an effort to please you and build intimacy. Assume there is no hidden agenda or sexual motive in this offer. If you suspect there is, ask. "Is this an offer for a back rub or an offer for a back rub that leads to sexual intercourse?" Believe the answer you get and respond according to your desires and wishes.

FIFTEEN THINGS TO
SAY TO BUILD CONNECTEDNESS

1. "Let's go for a walk."

2. "How about a heart-to-heart talk?"

3. "Let's go get an ice cream cone."

4. "Want to dance?"

5. "Let's light a couple of candles and
    turn off the lights."

6. "There's room for two under this afghan."

7. "Come here and I'll massage your feet."

8. "Let's go look at the stars."

9. "How about if we turn off the TV and have
    a little Prime Time of our own?"

10. "Want to reminisce?"

11. "How about if we drive out to Lovers'
    Lane and run out gas?"

12. "I love you."

13. "Want to use my shoulder?"

14. "Living with you has exceeded my
    wildest expectations."

15. "It doesn't get any better than this."

"LOG ON TO YOUR MARRIAGE DOT ORG."

"I love you."

REESE, A PRECOCIOUS SIX-YEAR-OLD, walked into the room and saw his mom and dad in a full embrace, kissing. "Hi, Mom and Dad, what are you guys doing?" he asked.

"I'm kissing your mother and holding her close," his father replied.

"You must really love her," Reese said.

"I do. Do you know why I do?" asked his father, still locked in an embracing hug.

With little thought, Reese replied, "You love Mom because she takes good care of you."

"No, that's not why," his dad replied.

"Is it because she's so cute?" Reese asked.

"No, it's . . ."

Before his dad could finish, Reese ventured another guess. "Because she's so kind and gentle?"

"Hold on," said his dad. "Think for a moment. Think about love. Why do I love you? Why does your mom love you? Do we love you because of the things you do, or because of who you are?"

Only a few seconds passed before Reese's face lit up with a smile. "You love me because I'm lovable."

"Yes!" his dad replied. "So why do you think I love your mom?"

"You love her because she's lovable," Reese answered.

"And sometimes I hug and kiss her because she's lovable," added his dad.

Reese smiled and bounced out of the room. His mom and dad pulled one another closer and kissed again.

What Reese was learning at an early age is that love is not about behavior. Love is not based on kindness, physical beauty, or task completion. Real love is unconditional and is based on simply being.

To many adults, love seems complicated and mysterious. Difficult to understand at times, love brings up feelings and thoughts that can be experienced in no other way. Some say love is blind. Others say it brings clarity. Some find it easy to love. Others struggle.

Whatever our interpretation of love, it is meant to be expressed as well as felt. People express love in a variety of ways. Some find it easiest to demonstrate their love materially. They enjoy giving their partners presents such as flowers, cards, candy, jewelry, and clothing. Others show their love by working hard to provide for their loved ones. They spend hours preparing a meal, keeping the house clean, or working overtime to pay the bills. These methods of showing love have a direct, visual/behavioral component.

Other people are drawn to physical expression, showing love in a tactile mode through touch. They communicate love with an embrace, a hug, handholding, or snuggling. Sex is another way love can be demonstrated in a tactile fashion.

Verbal expression is a third way to communicate love. Everyone likes to hear the words, "I love you." We recommend that you say it to each other often. An especially intimate form of "I love you" includes your partner's name. "Bethany, I love you." Tell your partner, "I love you, Fernando," and watch his reaction.

Your partner could *see* a visual demonstration of your love through the giving of gifts or through your willingness to provide. He could *feel* its manifestation as physical touch. He could *hear* its expression as you whisper the Couple Talk phrase, "I love you, Rocky." All three modes of expressing love are valuable.

Your partner may have a preferred way of receiving an "I love you" message. Use the method he or she most easily recognizes and responds to. She may like the active, behavioral expression best. He may prefer the tactile approach. Or perhaps the verbal will be his favorite. The "words of love" may be what he literally "hears" best.

But whatever method you choose as your preferred mode of expression, be sure that you balance it by using the other modes as well. Accompany your actions with words and your words with action.

If you choose to use the words "I love you" with your partner, don't make it conditional: "I love you *if* . . ." or "I love you *when* . . ." These forms of "I love you" indicate that your love is dependent upon your partner's behavior. If I love you when you work hard, what does it mean when you don't work hard? If I love you if you do what I want in bed, what happens to my love when you don't do what I want?

As Reese knows, you love someone because they are lovable *just the way they are*. Give love to your partner just because he or she is lovable. Your love is meant to be expressed. And it is meant to be heard and felt unconditionally.

HEARING

Be attentive to the many ways your partner has of saying "I love you." They may be sending messages of love more often than you realize. Sometimes they may use the actual words. Other times they may say it with a gift, a gentle touch, or a simple act of service.

"Make love to me."

ALICIA OPENED THE DOOR and stepped into the house after a long day at the office. Enrique, her husband, stood immediately inside the door, and he was smiling. As Alicia entered, Enrique whispered, "I talked to your sister and she took the kids for the night." He paused, and then added, "We have this night all to ourselves."

Alicia suspected what Enrique had in mind. She, too, had ideas for how to spend the evening. She stepped closer and whispered in her husband's ear, "I want you to make love to me tonight."

Enrique had heard his wife use this phrase before. He knew exactly what it meant. And he had accurately predicted she would use it again this evening. Holding her gently, he replied, "I have a hot bubble bath waiting for you upstairs. I'll put on some soft music and get a book to read while you climb into the tub. Take your time, Alicia. I'll be up in a moment."

As Alicia ascended the stairs, she smiled at the thought of a quiet evening with her husband. She could feel herself becoming excited. Although they had not yet kissed, their lovemaking had already begun.

"Make love to me" is not about sex. Nor is it about unbridled passion. It is a plea for tenderness and intimacy. When you say, "Make love to me," you are asking for kissing, touching, caressing, nuzzling, and lingering. It is a plea for a slow hand, softness, and admiring eyes.

When partners agree to "make love," the focus is on the process of love rather than on an orgasmic result. The process and the ritual of making love become the center of what you and your partner are sharing. Although "making love" may result in an orgasm for one or both parties, orgasm is not the goal. The goal is to enjoy the feeling of loving one another throughout the entire experience. This includes extended foreplay building up to the climax, staying close after the climax, and continuing to kiss and caress long after the orgasm is over.

Saying to your partner, "Make love to me," is sharing a want. It's OK to ask for what you want. It's healthy to ask for what you want. And that includes asking for sex if that happens to be your immediate desire.

If sex is what you want, say that. A simple, "Let's have sex," works well if you want to focus on the act of sex, with intercourse as the dominant activity. Or say, "I want to indulge my lust tonight." If you're feeling spontaneous, say, "I want a quickie." When you want to focus on your partner's desires, tell him, "I want to please you."

The object is to communicate your desires about sex. Say what you want, even if it's out of the ordinary or not typical for you. Saying what you're thinking or feeling removes the guesswork. When your partner knows what you want, you can work together to meet each other's desires.

HEARING

When your partner says, "Make love to me," refrain from hearing it as criticism of what you have done in the past. Hear it as a call for variation, for intimacy, for slowing down the pace. Hear him or her asking that the focus be on the process rather than on the orgasm. Hear their desire to have the softness and gentleness of a sexual encounter last the entire time.

Talking Dirty

JUSTIN AND BETH had been married for less than two years. They chose sexual abstinence during their year-long engagement and were now enjoying the satisfaction of a happy sex life full of love, intimacy, and passion. Their experiences of pleasing one another sexually were beyond enjoyable. As a couple they were growing into new levels of mutual excitement, experimentation, and trust.

One night, caught in the grip of passion, Justin used two phrases that had not yet been spoken during their lovemaking. Earthy in content and tone, the words that came out of his mouth surprised Justin himself, but an even greater surprise was Beth's reaction to his "dirty talk." She moaned when she heard the explicit language and squirmed beneath her husband, pressing her body upward in what seemed like an urgent attempt to get closer to the man who was talking to her with words she had never heard spoken in their marriage bed.

Justin detected a shift in Beth's breathing. It appeared to slow and become deeper. Encouraged, Justin repeated what he had said seconds earlier and embellished it by adding more "naughty" words. He was slightly embarrassed by his new language and felt a flush of self-consciousness flow through his body. He hoped that Beth wouldn't become disgusted.

Beth did not become disgusted. She became hot. Hot and wet. His wife totally forgot about "making love" in the moments that followed and threw herself into pure sex with reckless abandon. As Justin continued to whisper dirty words in her ear, Beth surrendered to her feelings of lust and clawed and scratched and screamed through what seemed to Justin like a fifteen-minute orgasm.

Justin didn't know for sure when Beth's climax began. And he wasn't quite sure when it ended. What he did know was that his wife had just completed one of the most sexually satisfying experiences of their married life. They both knew this would happen again soon.

Hattie and Preston began dating when both were in their late forties. Both were sexually experienced. They decided to have sex on their fifth date. They were planning to be married within six months.

One night, in the middle of intercourse, Hattie used the f-word. She used it several times in a row, commanding Preston to do what she wanted done. Surprised and unsure of how to respond, her partner hesitated. Again she used the f-word—this time louder—and this time she not only told him *what* she wanted done but *how* she wanted it done. Her description included the f-word and the phrase, "hard and deep."

Preston immediately went soft. Hattie's request for "hard and deep" had produced the opposite and undesired response of soft and shallow. Their lovemaking, like Preston's erection, came to an abrupt end.

Both couples spent a good portion of that night discussing sex and their feelings about talking dirty.

Talking dirty is not good or bad. It is not right or wrong. It is just talking dirty. What is important is how you and your partner feel about talking dirty and that you manage this issue with mutual respect.

Like oral sex, anal sex, or uncommon positions, talking dirty is only appropriate with the consent of your partner. Any act, position, or word is permitted in sexual play as long as there is mutual agreement. Expecting your partner to engage in an act or listen to words that offend them is not in the best interest of your partnership.

As with any sexual concern, talk with your partner about talking dirty. Check out their feelings ahead of time. See if you are close to agreement. Perhaps you'll agree to play with talking dirty—to check it out and see how it goes. Or maybe you'll agree that that type of language is not appropriate in your relationship in any way at any time. Each couple needs to pose and discuss the question of what is appropriate for them. Whatever answer you arrive at, respect it.

HEARING

If you hear dirty words in the middle of a sexual encounter, you have a choice. You can hear them as a playful attempt to heighten the sexual experience, as a slip that accidentally occurred in the heat of passion, or as a disgusting display of disrespect.

If you have negative feelings about the dirty talk, speak up immediately. Share them with your partner. Be as specific as possible. If it is just one or two specific words that you object to, tell your partner what they are. If you enjoy naughty language at certain times but not this time, then say that.

If you have positive feelings about the dirty talk, or are unsure of how you feel, you can wait until later to debrief. Monitor your feelings during the encounter. Notice what talking dirty does for your partner. Notice how you react to the experience.

When the sexual encounter has ended, debrief. Give your partner feedback. Listen to his or her views. Talking dirty may be Couple Talk that excites one or both of you, adding occasional variety to your sexual repertoire. Or it may be a complete turnoff that prevents sexual fulfillment for you or your partner. Decide together what works for you as a couple.

If you don't enjoy talking dirty and your partner does, hot sex talk may be a gift you can occasionally give them. Seeing the one you love excited and fulfilled brings a pleasure of its own. On the other hand, talking dirty may be a gift whose price is too steep for you to pay.

"**Let's do something weird.**"

"LET'S DO SOMETHING WEIRD" is a Couple Talk phrase that can add fun and adventure to your relationship—one that will remind you and your partner that a relationship can be more than problem-solving, conflict resolution, and struggle. It invites your partner to join you in discovering new and adventuresome ways to have fun together. It initiates grownup play. Similar phrases include:

"Come and be playful with me."

"Let's be adventurous."

"Let's be risky."

"Want to have some fun?"

"Let's step out of seriousness for a while."

"Can your 'kid' come out and play right now?"

The "something weird" could take many different forms—for example:

Playing in the rain and splashing in mud puddles

Going to a buffet and only eating from
the dessert table

Renting a type of movie you've
never watched before

"Watching" TV wearing blindfolds

Dressing up for Halloween and going
trick or treating together

Playing in the kids' sandbox when the
kids are not around

Having sex in a place different from where
you usually have it

Going for a drive and flipping a coin at each
corner to decide which way to turn next

"Let's do something weird" is about giving yourself
permission to do something unusual with your partner. It is a request to be the opposite of how we usually
are: serious, thoughtful, guarded, mature.

"Let's do something weird" can be the beginning
of an interesting dialogue. Brainstorming unusual,
fun ideas together could lead to exploring change. A
playful discussion could challenge you to use the
same Couple Talk communication skills you'd need if
you were discussing a much more serious issue. You
might find it fun to practice some of the skills you're
learning here on an issue that is far from life and
death importance.

One caution here: It's important to leave each
other an "out" if one of you is not enjoying the agreed-
upon adventure. Develop an escape clause, or an
"escape phrase," that can be used to stop the "fun"
when it no longer feels like fun for one of you.

Doing something weird and different can be a difficult stretch for some people. Give each other the
permission to stop when it stops being enjoyable.

Having fun is the main point of using this Couple Talk phrase. Keep the "fun" fun!

HEARING

When you hear your partner say, "Let's do something weird," remember that you're being invited to "come out and play." This invitation doesn't mean that things are not good enough in the relationship the way they are. Resist hearing that something is wrong. This is not an attempt to fix something that is broken. It is an effort to enhance what is already going pretty well.

Hear "Let's do something weird" as a request for a change of pace. Hear that your partner wants to do something different with you. Keep in mind that whatever it is he or she wants to do, they want to do it with you. Hear the request for your company as a compliment. Your partner loves and trusts you enough that they are willing to invite you to be weird with them.

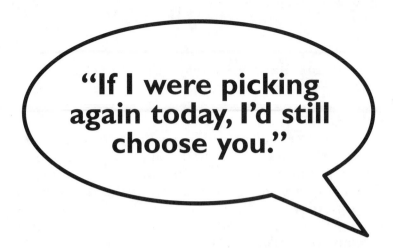

"If I were picking again today, I'd still choose you."

IMAGINE A COOL FALL EVENING. You're sitting on the porch swing with your spouse, huddled under an afghan, holding hands. Your wife leans closer, kisses your cheek, and says, "I just wanted you to know, if I were picking again today, I'd still choose you."

Do you feel the rush? Can you keep from smiling? Do you feel the urge to respond to the verbal hug with a physical one?

Every spouse needs to hear these or similar words on occasion. This kind of Couple Talk is affirming, nurturing, and appreciative. It is an intimate expression of love and caring that can generate warm feelings in both hearts.

"If I were picking again today, I'd still choose you" meets the needs of both parties. It helps the receiver feel valued and cherished. Simultaneously, it reminds the sender that she is at choice, that indeed every day is a choice, and that this day she still chooses the partner she picked many days, many months, or many years ago.

This phrase must come from the heart. Only say it if you know it to be true. It is not to be used for manipulation, to get sex, to make up, or to make yourself look good. If you don't mean it, don't say it.

If you can't say this phrase and mean it, ask yourself these questions: Am I sure that I'm where I want to be? How come I'm still in this relationship? What do I have to do, what changes need to be made, what thoughts, attitudes, and feelings need to change in order for me to be able to use this phrase and mean it?

If this phrase is not true, say what *is* true. If you have concerns about your relationship, share them. Communicate with an open heart, using the techniques and strategies explained in other portions of this book. If you have frustrations that need to be expressed, express them. If there is a problem that needs to be solved, bring it up.

By dealing with the issues that exist in your relationship in open, honest ways; by implementing the skills explained in this book; by facing the reality of your current situation in a solution-seeking stance, it may not be long before you'll be able to say with conviction, "If I were picking again today, I'd still choose you."

HEARING

Hear "If I were picking again today, I'd still choose you" as a compliment. Let it in. Feel it from the top of your head to the tip of your toes. Enjoy it. Give your partner a nonverbal response that lets them know how much you liked hearing those words. Do not feel obligated to respond in kind. If you want to, fine. Your partner would probably enjoy knowing that the feeling is mutual. "I'm really happy to hear that," accompanied by a hug, would be an appropriate response.

CHAPTER 4

The Language
of
Solution-Seeking

"Let's pick a time to talk about this."

As Juan unloaded his golf clubs from the trunk of the car, Maria noticed him putting a new club into his bag. "Where did you get that club?" she snapped.

"I've got to pick up Luis from soccer practice and I'm going to be late. Let's talk about it after I get back," Juan suggested.

Maria ignored Juan's request and kept on coming. "I'm not working overtime to pay the bills so you can blow it on a golf club!"

"I can't talk right now," Juan repeated.

"I'm not going to let you avoid this issue," Maria replied sternly.

Juan stepped closer, measured his words, and stated calmly, "Let's pick a time to talk about this. Let's talk about it in an hour, after I pick up Luis, unpack, and wash up."

Maria reluctantly agreed. She was angry and had a difficult time waiting a full hour. Although she smoldered silently about the issue, she knew Juan would talk to her as he said he would. This wasn't the first time one of them had used the Couple Talk phrase, "Let's set a time to talk about this." It had been her experience that whoever used the phrase followed through and talked about it on schedule.

True to his word, Juan picked up his son at soccer practice, cleaned up, collected his thoughts, and joined Maria in the living room.

"Maria," he began, "let me explain. The golf club isn't mine. It belongs to Charlie from the office. He bought it last week and had it regripped. He asked me to pick it up for him at the pro shop."

"Oh, I didn't know," Maria said, her tone soft and apologetic. I'm really sorry I jumped on you earlier."

Juan grabbed her hand and said, "It's OK. I know it looked like the club was mine. Let's spend a few minutes talking about the underlying concern—your overtime and our money situation."

"I don't want to talk about it right now. Let's talk about it at dinner tomorrow," Maria suggested.

"OK, tomorrow then," Juan replied.

Within an hour's time, both Juan and Maria had used the Couple Talk phrase, "Let's pick a time to talk about this." Each employed it as a useful tool to postpone a discussion when they were not ready to engage in a dialogue about the issue at hand. Each used it to communicate to their partner that they valued the concern being raised but that the timing needed to be changed. Each used it to honor their partner's agenda and to ask them to honor a different time frame.

Setting a time to discuss the issue allows both parties to relax, knowing they will get a chance to address the concern at a specified time. This eliminates the tendency to worry about the topic being avoided and never addressed.

The key to this Couple Talk skill is that you both talk about the issue at the time you agreed to do so. "Let's pick a time to talk about this" is not to be used as an avoidance tactic. It is a phrase of respect. Respect of the issue and respect of the timing.

You may find that your day or week is so busy that you actually need to schedule time with your partner on a regular basis. Neither of you may have any issues to address at the beginning of the week, but with a scheduled time for dealing with concerns, you both know issues won't get buried or forgotten if something does arise. If you get to the scheduled time and nobody has anything to discuss, great. That time can then be used to implement other strategies to stay connected and strengthen your relationship.

HEARING

Hear "Let's pick a time to talk about this" as a request to change the timing of the discussion, not as a request to change or avoid the issue. Hear it as an honest attempt to communicate a problem at a more appropriate time rather that as an effort to dodge it.

Pay attention to your partner's plea. She may be too deep in thought or too angry to think clearly at the moment, or she may simply need more time to think through her position on the matter. When you hear this phrase, remember that your partner wants to talk about the issue that concerns you and wants to be in the best frame of mind when doing so. She cares enough about the topic to want to pick a time where she can give it her full attention.

Hearing this phrase requires you to put your feelings of immediacy aside. Not everything needs to be addressed here and now. Remember, your partner may not be ready to talk about something at exactly the same time you are. Remain open to returning to the issue at a time that works for both of you.

"Let's make a plan."

"Let's create an adventurous vacation."

"How about if we design the way we would
like the new room to look?"

"Let's develop a plan for dealing with this child."

PLANNING IS ONE ACTIVITY in which healthy couples
engage. They invest time in exploring each other's
desires, interests, and goals. They create a plan together and reach consensus. They make their plan
concrete, verbalize it, and often put it in writing.

Sometimes the planning takes on the flavor of
problem-solving: *How can we arrange your mother's visit
to meet everyone's needs?* Other times it merely focuses
on alternatives: *What are some possibilities here? Let's
make a list.* Goal-setting can be the focal point of productive planning: *What goal shall we create for our use of
this Couple Talk material?* The planning conversation
could concentrate on dreams or fantasies: *What would
our dream house look like?* or *Where do we want to be ten
years from now?*

Does your Couple Talk include "Let's make a plan"? If not, why not create a plan to add it to your verbal repertoire?

HEARING

"Let's make a plan" is an invitation to become involved with your partner. Hear it as an opportunity to connect and to steer your partnership in a direction that is mutually satisfying and rewarding.

"Let's take a time-out."

BONITA NOTICED the volume increase in her own voice first. A few moments later she heard cutting comments coming from her husband, Henry. Bonita didn't wait for a third signal. She immediately employed a Couple Talk phrase intended to keep the situation from escalating out of control. "Let's take a time-out," she suggested.

Use "Let's take a time-out" if you believe a conversation is heading toward dangerous territory. Use it if frustration is threatening to obliterate listening. Use it if you suspect you might say something that you would later regret.

"Let's take a time-out" means exactly what it says—taking time away from dealing with the issue. It is a plea to back off, create some space, and cool down. While a time-out can be used to refocus and ponder the issue at hand, its main purpose is to regain self-control.

"Let's take a time-out" is not to be used as a delay or avoidance technique. It is not an escape mechanism that signals an end to communication about the concern in question. Taking a time-out means there will be a time-in. A mutually agreed upon time-out means: We are coming back to this issue. The problem will be dealt with when solution-seeking can be most productive—when we are both working against the problem and not against each other.

Great basketball coaches know when to call a time-out. They do it when their team has lost their composure or focus. They do it if their players are not using the skills learned in practice. They do it if their team members appear to have forgotten the game plan.

Follow the lead of successful basketball coaches. Call a time-out if you or your partner has lost your composure, are not using the skills learned in practice, or seem to have forgotten the game plan.

HEARING

When your partner calls for a time-out, honor it. Hear that they feel, hear, or see something that is leading to danger in your relationship. Know that while they are standing up for themselves by expressing their need, they are also standing up for the relationship.

Hear "Let's take a time-out" as a call for help. Trust that your partner knows what they need. Help them and yourself by joining with them in this effort to create an atmosphere that is conducive to solution-seeking.

A time-out is observed together. While you may be in separate rooms during the time-out, you and your partner are doing it together for the good of the relationship. This momentary separation is actually an act of joining. Hear the call for a time-out as a plea to join in an act that will benefit your relationship.

"Let's check it out inside."

MARY AND ALLAN were thinking of buying a house. They talked to realtors, bankers, relatives, and coworkers. They read books, searched the Internet, and studied interest trends. They listed and debated pluses and minuses. They evaluated, appraised, and analyzed.

Still, they weren't sure what to do. Confused and temporarily paralyzed, they lingered in a state of indecision until Mary suggested, "Let's check it out inside."

"Let's check it out inside" is a Couple Talk phrase that helps us remember to look within for answers. Each of us has a wise part within, an intuitive part that knows what is best for us. This inner knowing is invaluable when life presents us with problems whose answers aren't in the back of the book.

Mary and Allan turned off the television, lit two candles, and dimmed the lights. As they had done several times before in their marriage, they sat silently, connecting with their inner feelings. They did not use this time for thinking. Time for analyzing and study was over. This was a time to get out of their heads and into their hearts.

After fifteen minutes, Allan spoke. "I want to buy that house," he said. Mary nodded in agreement. They knew. And they knew they knew. And they trusted that knowing.

This inner knowing that Mary and Allan activated has been called by a variety of names. We've heard it referred to as "inner knowing," "gut-level feeling," "conscience," "intuition," "talking to God," and "the wise part within." What you choose to call it is not as important as learning how and when to use it.

"Let's check it out inside" is a statement of self-trust. It's an admission that there is much more to wisdom than merely logic. It's a decision to consider all the data when making a decision—data that comes from the inside as well as the outside.

HEARING

Hear "Let's check it out inside" as an invitation to consult your inner authority. Hear it as an opportunity to get out of your mind and feel your feelings. Hear it as a chance to access that wise part within you and put it to use in your life.

"If this was about
something else, what
would it be about?"

ANGER, FEAR, JEALOUSY, frustration, sadness, and other emotions manifest in many ways in our lives—sometimes in ways we do not immediately recognize. They often appear disguised in everyday issues, hidden from our consciousness by the outside events in which we wrap them. That's what happened to Sam and Cathy recently.

Sam liked to stop on the way home from work occasionally and drink beer with his friends. Sometimes he would stay longer than he intended. Always he spent money. And he always came home. An argument usually followed.

Cathy, full of anger, would vent her frustration in loud accusation. Her arguments centered on the money Sam spent, often between fifty and seventy-five dollars. Sam countered that he had plenty of money, retirement savings were abundant, and his paycheck was generous. Both parties were correct and both appeared right in their own minds.

The money wars raged for several months until a thought occurred to Sam in the middle of the now-familiar argument. "If this argument wasn't about money," he asked, "if this was about something else, what would it be about?"

What Sam had done with his "If this wasn't about money" question was to call a time-out and ask for a shift in perception. He was asking Cathy, as well as himself, to dig deeper, to peel off a layer of their anger, to move past the surface to a deeper level.

In this case, the "What are we really mad about?" discussion led to greater understanding and resolution. Cathy was able to access her feelings of insecurity about not knowing where Sam was when he didn't come home. It became apparent that the feelings were left-over hurt from her latchkey days as a child—the insecurity of not knowing where her parents were and when they would come home—and they were triggered anew by Sam's behavior.

Once the real reason for the anger surfaced, Sam and Cathy were able to find a solution that satisfied both their needs. Sam called Cathy before he stopped and set an exact time at which he would be home. He got to be with his friends on occasion and Cathy was secure in knowing where her husband was and when he would be home.

"What else is this like?"

"Where else have we felt these feelings?"

"What are we really mad about?"

"If we knew what else this is about,
what would it be?"

Questions like these can help us take a step back in the middle of a negative manifestation of behavior. They allow us a time-out moment to reflect and reconsider the events unfolding around us. They permit us to call forth a new perspective, a deeper understanding, a new insight. They can help us see and experience things differently.

Lattrell Wilson asked, "If this was about something else, what would it be about?" as he felt his anger mount over his young child's lack of table manners. He discovered that the anger was not about eating patterns at all but about his feeling of being out of control with his child. With that discovery, Lattrell was able to work more effectively on his control issues as well as on his child's table manners.

Chad Kreuter got irritated with his wife Betsy because she wasn't following him correctly on the dance floor. The man leads. The woman follows. That's the way it is in dancing, he thought to himself, justifying his irritation at his wife's failure to follow his lead. When Betsy raised the question, "If this was about something else, what would it be about?" later that evening, the real issue surfaced—sex.

The rest of the evening was devoted to exploring the feelings both parties had about how sex was handled in their relationship. The discussion improved both their sex lives and their dancing.

In the middle of an argument and not sure what it's about? Feeling what seems like an overreaction to an event or circumstance? Noticing an intense feeling about a familiar situation? Are you getting really angry as you read these pages? If so, why not ask, "If this was about something else, what would it be about?"

HEARING

When you hear, "If this was about something else, what would it be about?" take the question seriously. Stop long enough to contemplate the question. Dig deep. Maybe the argument that you're having is really about another issue.

What your partner is really saying is, I don't believe this topic can be creating this much energy in us. Could it be about something else? Back up. Look at the issue again from a different perspective. You might be surprised by what you discover.

"Let's turn
our binoculars
around."

DURING A COUPLE TALK WEEKEND RETREAT, people were asked to make a list of the issues they frequently fought about with their partner. This is a list of the most common responses.

Spending time with extended family
during the holidays

Putting the toilet seat down

Leaving material from work in piles
on the kitchen table

Frequency of sex

Leaving lights on in the house when
no one is home

Not cleaning up the kitchen after getting
something to eat

Leaving dirty clothes on the floor next
to the laundry basket

Money and how it is spent

Disciplining children

Amount of family time

Control of the thermostat

Each couple was asked to pick one issue on which to focus. The group leader then asked participants to create make-believe binoculars by making two loose fists and putting them in front of their eyes. They were then instructed to look through the binoculars and focus on the disagreement under consideration. They were asked to use their binoculars to bring the situation up close and examine it in detail. Partners were encouraged to talk to each other about their sightings using their high-powered imaginary binoculars. Later, they were asked to report their experiences to the total group.

"I got really angry," one person said. "I could clearly see the thermostat set at 71 and 3/4 degrees. The heat was passing through the walls. My temperature was rising, too."

Other comments included:

"I could focus up real close on the clock. It was after midnight and she wasn't home yet."

"I could see her dad eating, and his table manners were atrocious as usual."

"I saw ants marching through the living room, heading for the food scraps."

"The toilet seat came into view and it was in the wrong position. I could almost see his fingerprints on it."

The comments were intense. So were the feelings generated by the view through the imaginary binoculars. It was almost as if the closer people got to the issue, the stronger they felt about it. Interestingly, the more intense the feeling, the more difficulty the participants had communicating with their partners.

The workshop leader then asked participants to pick up their pretend binoculars again. Only this time he asked them to turn the binoculars around. "Remember," he cautioned, "when you look through binoculars this way, you reverse the magnification, and everything you see is smaller." Participants were encouraged to view the same situation they examined earlier from this broader perspective.

Attendees' responses to the experience varied greatly from the previous look through the binoculars. This time they reported:

"The situation seemed so far away. It didn't seem all that important."

"It helped me see money as part of a bigger picture."

"I realized there are more important things than dirty laundry."

By slightly shifting their perspective, many of the couples were able to reduce the intensity of their feelings around the issue at hand and begin to talk about it more effectively. The term we use to describe this shift in perception is "turning your binoculars around."

A strategy similar to turning your binoculars around is to think about how you might feel about the issue ten years from now, twenty-five years from now, even one hundred years from now. How important is this issue in all of time? Ask yourself what this issue would look like if you were to take a step back and look at it from a distance. If it wouldn't matter ten years from now, is it worth fighting about today?

By taking the opportunity to turn your binoculars around or create a mental time warp, you change your perspective. And in relationships, perspective is everything. It is not so much what happens to you that affects how you feel, but *how you perceive* what happens to you.

Each of us chooses how to view a given situation. The event does not control how we perceive it. We are in charge of our own perceptions. We control how we see the event.

If you're having trouble dealing with a specific relationship issue, shift your perspective and invite your partner to join you by saying, "Let's turn our binoculars around." Use this Couple Talk phrase to remind yourself to take control of how you perceive an issue. In terms of all of time, how big is this problem, really? Turn your binoculars around and reap the benefits of creating your own perception.

HEARING

When you hear your partner suggest, "Let's turn our binoculars around," ask yourself: Am I making a mountain out of a molehill? Your partner is calling on you to shift your perspective—to change the magnifying lens through which you see this event. They are giving you the opportunity to check within yourself to see if you really think this is worth the time and effort you're putting into it. They are asking, Do you want to get up close and make this issue big, or do you want to stand at a distance and make it appear smaller?

"Is this worth fighting about?"

DELBERT AND CORETTA had a bitter argument over
whether or not the checkbook was balanced regularly
and accurately. Simon and Brenda fought about how
often they visited each person's mother. Jasper and
Roger got into a heated discussion about the type of
food they were feeding their dog. Both parties in each
scenario went to bed mad.

In each case the fight didn't seem that important
the next day. With the benefit of hindsight, all three
couples agreed that the issue that had separated them
the evening before was unimportant. Each member
admitted they cared more about feelings of connectedness, love, and maintaining a positive relationship
than they did about the issue that had divided them.

"Is this worth fighting about?" asks both you and
your partner to become conscious of the issue at hand.
It asks each of you to consider: How important is this
to me, really? Is it more important than connectedness? Is it more important than a loving evening at
home? Does the value of this disagreement exceed
that of harmony and peace?

"Is this worth fighting about?" is a Couple Talk
phrase that, asked in the middle of an argument,

could save you and your partner time, energy, and hurt feelings. If the agreed-upon answer is no, the issue can be resolved quickly. The rest of the day can then take on new direction.

The answer to "Is this worth fighting about?" could be yes. It is possible that either you or your partner may feel the issue is extremely important and choose to continue the struggle. In that case, the argument can resume with the added insight that its importance has been validated by at least one of you. If the person who cares deeply about the concern shares why they feel as they do, further data is brought to the discussion that may help resolve it.

Fighting is not necessarily a bad thing—nor is arguing. What is unhealthy to the relationship is if the argument stays unresolved, if participants fight unfairly, without clean, clear communication, or if the parties do not make up later. A lack of closure to an argument or fight can have more disastrous results than the fight itself.

HEARING

"Is this worth fighting about?" is a signal from your partner. He or she is telling you that the concern that divides you doesn't seem that important to them and they want to find out how important it is to you.

"Is this worth fighting about?" sounds like a question. It is not. It is a statement that your relationship is more important to your partner than the issue is. They care so much about you and the relationship that they want to hear exactly how you feel about the issue under discussion and how important it is to you.

"How can we both get what we want?"

CARLOS WANTED A BIG WEDDING. Carmen wanted a small one. Neither was willing to budge. Although the couple had been engaged for over a year and sincerely wanted to marry, the wedding date kept getting pushed back.

The big wedding/small wedding discussion took place frequently, but without resolution. Then one day Carlos asked, "Is there a way we can both get what we want?"

"What do you mean?" his fiancée responded.

"Let's talk about what we really want and see if we can't put our wants together somehow."

Carmen agreed, and within an hour they had forged a happy solution to the troubling dilemma.

Carlos wanted a big wedding because he had lots of friends and family members who wanted to party. He didn't want to disappoint them and needed a big wedding so he could throw a huge bash.

Carmen wanted the sacredness of a small wedding attended by family and a few close friends. She wanted the tradition of a small chapel with an emphasis on spirituality and a union created and blessed by God.

Their solution? A small, intimate wedding and a huge reception. Both needs met. Both people happy.

Couples in conflict usually focus on "winning" an argument because experience has taught them that compromise often means giving up what you want. Compromise means that everyone loses something.

"How can we both get what we want?" will help you redefine problems in terms of wants and needs instead of winners and losers. It will open up options where previously there seemed to be none. It will encourage cooperation so both parties can win.

Stuck with a problem? Why not ask, "How can we both get what we want?"

HEARING

"How can we both get what we want?" is an invitation to explore the situation in terms of wants and needs. Your partner is suggesting you work together to solve the problem in a way that both of you win. He or she does not want to lose, nor do they want to see you lose. Consider the offer to work together to redefine the problem and search for a solution that is acceptable to both of you.

"WHEN I SAID I WANTED TO GO OUT TO EAT, I MEANT FARTHER OUT."

"Can we present
a united front
on this?"

ARMON AND KRISTA WERE WAITING for their teenage
son to return home. He was forty-five minutes late.
This was the third time he had been out past curfew.
Krista looked at Armon and asked, "Can we present a
united front on how to handle this?"

Brenda and Art discussed the upcoming holiday
season and how they would handle dividing their time
between her relatives and his. They agreed on a plan
to balance the visiting time evenly between both sides
of the family. As the discussion wound down, Art suggested, "When we talk about this plan with our
families, let's present a united front."

Charles and Nan were on their way to a meeting
with the principal at their son's school. Charles Jr. had
been complaining about the teacher's use of the term
"Shut up" in the classroom. Each parent had a different feeling about the situation, as well as an opinion
about what needed to be done. As the couple pulled
up in front of the school, Nan turned to Charles and
said, "Before we go in to meet the principal, let's talk
briefly about presenting a united front."

Each couple in the above scenarios had a problem
to solve that involved a third party. Each needed to

create and demonstrate solidarity. To produce that solidarity, each used a variation of the highly effective Couple Talk strategy, "Can we present a united front on this?"

Disagreement is common between partners in a relationship. No two people consistently have the same perspective on things. Contrasting points of view arise. Attitudes conflict. Differences of opinion occur. All of this is natural and to be expected in an evolving relationship between two distinct individuals.

Many couples become immobilized when faced with disagreement and differing opinions. They become disconnected as each person struggles to defend and uphold their own personal position. Harmony, symmetry, and connectedness are often compromised. And, worst of all, partners frequently allow their differences to result in no action at all being taken.

"Can we present a united front on this?" is a call for action—unified action. The goal is for both parties to act as one when addressing the issue, whether agreement between them has been reached or not. To present a united front it is necessary to find a place to stand together in the midst of conflict, differences, and disagreement. That common ground could be respect and concern for one another, making sure the other's point of view is understood, or following through on an agreed-upon plan. Or it might simply be focusing on staying connected rather than on the disagreement.

Armon and Krista created a united front by agreeing on a disciplinary approach that they could both support and implement. When their son arrived home, they stood together as they announced the consequences.

Brenda and Art stood on common ground as they followed through with their plan for the holidays. Together they addressed their families, and neither backed down when pressured by family members to alter their plans.

Charles and Nan each concisely presented their individual concerns to the principal. Their united front was established by supporting each other's thoughts and feelings as they were offered.

What will you do when you can't agree with your partner? Will you allow differences of opinion to result in disconnection? Will you yield to contrasting viewpoints and compromise your harmony? Will you defend your position to the point of risking unity? Or will you consider putting harmony into action by asking, "Can we present a unified front on this?"

HEARING

When you hear your partner ask, "Can we present a united front on this?" hear his or her desire for unity. Your partner wants to stay connected as you move through the current issue. He or she is calling you to join them in spirit and in action. Hear the desire for harmony rather than for disharmony. Look past the disagreement. Focus on staying connected. Search for common ground and stand together.

"Can we agree
to disagree?"

JASON CALLS IT "SMOTHERING." Anita says it's "mother-ing." She thinks she is being helpful. Jason thinks she is rescuing. Differing opinions on this parenting issue have existed for this couple since the birth of their son four years ago. Recently, Jason and Anita quit arguing about this aspect of parenting. Instead, they agreed to disagree.

Some issues exist in every relationship that will never be agreed upon. It could be how often you have sex, what consequences you provide for misbe-having children, or how many dollars you allocate from your budget for fun and entertainment. Reaching a consensus in these cases is unlikely because arriv-ing at an agreement would require one person to cave in and behave in ways that go against their basic beliefs. No one likes, nor should anyone be required, to sacrifice his or her core beliefs simply for the sake of agreement.

"Can we agree to disagree?" is Couple Talk that offers a way out of this dilemma. It suggests an alter-native way to reach a consensus, one that allows both parties to maintain their beliefs. You can agree that you don't see the issue the same way. You can agree that neither of you is likely to switch sides. You can agree that the issue will probably remain unresolved. You can agree to disagree.

Continuing to argue about issues that won't go away is a waste of time. So is working to convince your partner of your superior logic in these situations. You believe that smoking is harmful. Your spouse believes that smoking a cigar now and then causes no harm. Good luck trying to get the other to change their mind.

Lack of agreement does not mean that your relationship is doomed. It does not mean that you have poor solution-seeking skills. It does not mean that you need to sign up for six weeks of conflict resolution classes. It does not mean that counseling is necessary. It means only that you have no agreement on this issue.

Agreeing to disagree helps you to transcend the conflict. It places your relationship above the issue, putting more importance on acknowledging and accepting each other's beliefs than on making one party right and the other wrong. This attitude results in less insult, less judgment, and fewer inferences about one another.

Not all conflicts end with closure on the issue at hand. Nor do they need to. It isn't necessary to keep arguing, using conflict resolution strategies, searching for solutions until a tidy package of consensus is painfully forged. What is important is that you achieve emotional closure. Agreeing to disagree will help you reach a common ground on the issue so you can reconnect emotionally.

HEARING

When your partner uses the words, "Let's agree to disagree," know that they have given up attempting to convince you. He or she has realized that you are not going to convince them. They are telling you that you may both have to accept the fact that there will be no agreement on this issue.

"**Let's focus on your complaint.**"

Husband: "I could use some more attention, some kind words, some appreciation."

Wife: "You're not the only one who does things that are unnoticed around here. I could use more help with the children and the laundry. How come you never do that?"

Husband: "You spend so much time with your friends. That's why the house is messy all the time and you don't get your work done. If you cared as much about us as you do about your friends, things would be a lot better around here."

Wife: "I suppose you think that *your* friends are wonderful. Your pal, Jason, flirts with me every time he comes over. Don't you see the way he looks at me? I don't understand why you keep bringing him around to gawk at me."

Husband: "You bring it on. The way you dress around my friends is ridiculous. You still try to look like a teenager. Why don't you get some new clothes that fit?"

Wife: "If you gave me more money for clothes, I could dress better. If you'd stop smoking, we'd have some extra money. Then maybe I could get some nice things."

Husband: "You go through money like it was water. What about that money you spend on massages? Is that really necessary?"

This couple is caught in the game of counter-complaining. This kind of interaction happens when each party answers a complaint with a complaint. Sometimes counter-complaining takes the form of restating and summarizing one's original complaint. Other times, a fresh complaint is added with each response. Either way, no listening, no understanding, and no resolution occur.

The counter-complaining merry-go-round will continue until someone breaks the cycle. Someone has to decide to end it by focusing on one complaint at a time. Until that decision is made and acted upon, counter-complaining will be counter-productive.

"Let's focus on that concern" is Couple Talk that signals an attempt to focus on understanding the other's point of view. It announces a shift from pressing a point to listening for a point. "Let's concentrate on your complaint," "How about if we deal with the flirting issue for a while?" or "Help me understand that concern" are ways to break the counter-complaint cycle.

Summarizing the other's position is another way to use verbal skills to break out of the counter-complaint game. "So it sounds as though you have some concerns about the amount of time I spend with Kelly and Deb. You wish I would put that time into keeping the house clean." Summarizing the other's position at any point in the game will usually turn the conversation toward solution-seeking. Summarizing breaks the pattern of counter-complaining by halting the flow of complaints. When the complaint flow stops, it is possible to concentrate on one issue at a time and move toward understanding and resolution.

It only takes one person to end the counter-complaint game. We suggest that the person who recognizes it first be the one to make the move. Resist pressing your point. Turn your efforts from convincing to understanding. Tell your partner, "Let's focus on your complaint."

Hearing

Hear "Let's focus on your complaint" as an invitation to get off the counter-complaint merry-go-round. Your partner is prepared to listen and consider your complaint. He or she is willing to hold their complaints until this one has been processed.

If you accept the invitation, confine your remarks to only one issue. State it as clearly as possible, helping your partner reach understanding. Remember, understanding and agreeing are not always synonymous. Even if resolution remains elusive, working on one issue at a time will strengthen your communication style and your relationship.

"What can we learn from this?"

TYRONE AND JILLIAN WERE CELEBRATING their twelfth wedding anniversary with a dinner at a five-star restaurant. The children were home with Grandma and they had a romantic evening ahead of them. Tyrone ordered a bottle of wine to celebrate. The meal was tasty and the conversation intimate and a bit naughty. On the way home in the car, Jillian put on some of their favorite music.

It was a wonderful anniversary celebration—wonderful until the flashing lights of a police car broke the spell of romance. Tyrone received a ticket for failing to make a complete stop and another for driving while under the influence of alcohol.

After a long evening at the police station, Jillian sat down across from Tyrone at the kitchen table and asked, "What can we learn from this?"

Jake took pictures at his son's church youth group outing. He snapped pictures of everyone in sight. His plan was to have the pictures developed at a one-hour photo lab so they would be ready the next day for viewing at church.

When Jake shared the photos at Sunday school the following day, he received many compliments.

Everyone seemed to think the pictures were great. But later that week, the pastor called him. Some of the high school girls had reported being uncomfortable with Jake taking their picture. They accused him of taking inappropriate photos of their breasts and bottoms. Jake was stunned and hurt. The accusations were far from the truth. He had the negatives to prove it.

Angry and embarrassed, Jake shared the incident with his wife, Molly. After listening thoroughly and honoring her husband's feelings, Molly asked, "What can we learn from this?"

Mistakes and misunderstandings happen in every relationship. They are a fact of life. Sometimes the infractions are minor. Other times the mistakes are so big the results are tragic. Regardless of their intensity and impact, mistakes happen for a reason. They occur so we can learn lessons, so we can grow and move on with our lives, wiser and better able to handle what comes our way.

"What can we learn from this?" is pivotal Couple Talk in the wake of a mistake or misunderstanding. It prompts a pivot turn away from dwelling on the mistake and moves a couple in the direction of learning from it. Often a lesson comes disguised as a mistake or misunderstanding.

Asking "What can we learn from this?" puts an end to finding fault and judging one another. It puts you and your partner on the same side, facing the problem together, focusing your energy on moving forward. It helps you search for lessons rather than for someone to blame.

A key word in "What can we learn from this?" is *we*. When you sit down with your partner to explore the learning opportunities hidden in a mistake, there are three areas to examine: what "I" learned, what "you" learned, and what "we" learned.

Each person has a unique perspective that influences what he or she learns in any given situation. The "we" part is about how you put your individual perspectives together and consider what your relationship has to learn. The "what we learned" portion calls you to look past yourself, past your partner, and into the partnership, into the relationship.

Use your mistakes to your own advantage. Be willing to learn and grow from them. Turn your mistakes and misunderstandings into learning opportunities by asking, "What can we learn from this?"

HEARING

Hear "What can we learn from this?" as a liberating statement. You are liberated from being shamed and berated for your mistakes. You are liberated from the pressure to never make a mistake. Hear that your partner is willing to work with you and learn from mistakes—both yours and theirs.

Remember, mistakes will affect your relationship. Exactly how depends on the lessons learned.

**"...AND TO THINK WE'VE BEEN
ATTENDING COUPLE TALK CLASSES."**

**"What would
love do now?"**

WHEN MAKING AN IMPORTANT DECISION, couples consider a variety of criteria. Will we regret this later?
How much money will it cost us? Will we get anything
back? Will it be worth our time and effort? Will this
commit us to anything else? Will it affect our lifestyle?
Will we win or lose? Will we look good? What will we
have to give up? What impact will this have on our
time? How badly do we want to do this? Will this be
something that will bring pleasure? Will we get any
recognition?

Couples whose main purpose in being a couple is
to help and support each other in growing spiritually often ask a different question than those posed
above. When faced with a dilemma and unsure about
what to do, they find it useful to ask, "What would love
do now?"

There is no question more important to the spiritual development of you and your partner than "What
would love do now?" If your reason for being together
is to accumulate a healthy retirement portfolio, climb
the corporate ladder, build fame and recognition, or
hold on to what you have, then this question need not

be part of your Couple Talk. If, on the other hand, Spirit is your goal, the most meaningful, relevant, helpful question you can ask in any situation is, "What would love do now?"

Barb and Lenny struggled with what to do with their delinquent teenage son. He disobeyed family rules. He came home whenever he felt like it, smoked dope in the house, and spoke disrespectfully to his mother. Barb and Lenny had recently been to a series of Tough Love meetings and were seriously considering barring their son from their home.

Brenda's aged mother had been living with Brenda and her husband, Richard, for six years. A recent downturn in the elderly woman's health had the pair considering a nursing home for their valued and beloved family member.

In each case it was the husband who verbalized the Couple Talk question, "What would love do now?" Both couples had used the question to make decisions in the past. They were more than familiar with the spiritual criteria at the center of this question. Loving, growing in spirit, and living from that essence had become the central focus of their coming together, living together, and staying together.

After asking themselves, "What would love do now?" Brenda and Richard decided against a retirement home for Brenda's mother. They sold their timeshare vacation properties, put their retirement plans on hold, and hired a live-in nurse to handle evenings.

Brenda and Richard did not make this decision out of a sense of obligation. They did not do it because it was the "right" thing to do. They did not base it on what people at their church might think. They decided that love would welcome the opportunity for mutual growth and fulfillment that this situation provided. They loved themselves and each other enough to take this opportunity to give and thus receive more love.

After considering "What would love do now?" Barb and Lenny evicted their son from their home. They concluded that loving their son did not mean letting him do whatever he wished. They determined that the best way they could demonstrate their love would be to draw boundaries, make those boundaries clear, and then hold to them. Loving their son meant they would hold him accountable for the choices he made and give him an opportunity to learn about cause and effect. Loving themselves meant they would not allow themselves to be walked on or permit their boundaries to be violated without immediate consequences being implemented.

"What would love do now?" does not have to be used exclusively for heavy-duty issues like tough love and nursing home decisions. It can be used to determine how you and your partner budget your money, choose who to invite to a party, or decide whether or not your daughter goes to summer camp. You can use it to help decide if you should join a church committee, take dance lessons together, or give this book to a friend.

Other ways to ask, "What would love do now?" include:

"What would Christ do in this situation?"

"How would the Buddha handle this?"

"How do you think Muhammad would respond to this?"

"What reaction would the Dali Lama have?"

Look for an opportunity to use "What would love do now?" during the next week. Find a situation and play with it, using one of these questions. Try it on for size. See if it fits. Later, debrief. Determine whether or not this Couple Talk skill can serve you in the future.

HEARING

If your partner asks, "What would love do now?" he or she is suggesting that you put spirituality into the equation of deciding how to handle the situation before you. They are saying that helping each other grow spiritually is a primary purpose of your relationship as they see it. They are inviting you to participate in the adventure of living a relationship that places spiritual growth first.

"Let's talk
about how we
talked about it."

KATHY AND CAROLYN HAD BEEN A COUPLE for over three years. Like most couples, they had disagreements and misunderstandings that needed to be brought to consciousness and worked through from time to time. Friday night was one of those times.

Carolyn discovered that Kathy had been reading her private e-mail. Furious, Carolyn shared her feelings, triggering a three-hour discussion. During the argument which ensued, voices were raised and then lowered, tempers were lost and then found, egos were bruised and then soothed. The emotional temperature fluctuated widely.

The discussion, which included an honest reporting of feelings and desires, ended with a solution acceptable to both parties. Friday night was salvaged, the weekend was saved, and the relationship moved on. On Sunday night, Carolyn suggested, "Let's talk about how we talked about it."

Note that Carolyn did not recommend, "Let's talk about how the solution is working." Her invitation was not to examine the particular solution they arrived at or the reason they needed it in the first place. She was asking to talk about the process that she and her partner went through to arrive at the solution.

Yes, the solution is important. So is whether or not it is working. The effectiveness of the solution clearly needs to be examined. That will occur at a later date during a separate discussion. This discussion is intended to examine only how the parties arrived at the solution.

"Let's talk about how we talked about it" is an offer to debrief the process that led to the solution. Issues to be looked at here could include: Were we respectful to one another? Did we use our Couple Talk skills? Did we listen actively? Did we fight fair? Did we hold anything back? Did we browbeat? Did we each get what we wanted without damaging the relationship?

Effective debriefing helps us celebrate our successes. What parts did we do well? What can we pat ourselves on the back for? What do we like about how we treated each other? Debriefing can help us improve. What do we need to work on? What would we do differently next time? What would be a helpful growth area for us?

The greatest solution in the world is not good enough if the participants are mean to each other in the process of creating it. The process that is used when handling conflict is more important than the result that it produces. Debriefing helps each person involved stay conscious of that process so that it can be continually strengthened, along with the relationship.

HEARING

"Let's talk about how we talked about it" is an invitation to participate in examining and strengthening the communication process. Your partner is telling you that how you work things out is important to him or her. Hear their suggestion as an opportunity to work together on how you work together.

Although debriefing is a serious endeavor, upon completion of talking about how you talked about it, throw in some humor. Invite your partner to talk about how you talked about talking about it. Or maybe not.

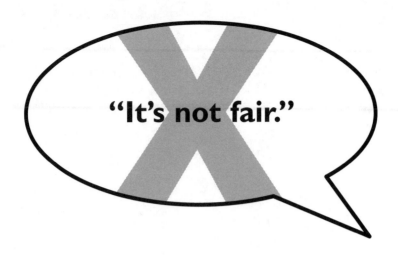

"I'm always the one who has to get up with the kids
in the middle of the night. It's not fair."

"You get to stop on the way home from work
and have a drink with your friends, while I'm
at home with the kids. That's not fair."

"It's not fair that I have to make all
the money around here."

"You seem to have the time for your hobby.
It's only fair that I get time for mine."

"It's not fair that you're in charge of
the checkbook."

"The fair thing to do would be to let me
have the new car this week."

"It's not fair that we always go to your
parents' house for the holidays."

AT ONE TIME or another we have all heard, and
maybe even uttered, the familiar words, "It's not fair."
In times of perceived injustice, the phrase just seems
to roll off our tongues.

"It's not fair" is used in an attempt to bring balance to an area of perceived imbalance, to right a wrong, or to shame a partner into changing so we get our needs met. It's a form of manipulation.

Common as the phrase may be, "It's not fair" is Couple Talk that is based on a faulty core belief—the belief that life is and should be fair at all times. The unrealistic expectation at the center of this belief is that I should have the same as everyone else because that is what's right.

We all know that, in reality, life is not fair. Two people can be speeding down the highway and only one gets stopped and ticketed. Two people can be exposed to the same virus and only one of them becomes sick. Prosperity comes to some while seeming to pass others by. Consequences for crimes committed are not levied equitably in all cases. Loopholes in the tax system are used by some and never discovered by others. The reality is that one cannot expect that fairness will be applied to them at all times and in all cases. It just isn't going to happen.

"It's not fair" is victim language. It says, Poor me, ain't it awful. It sounds whiny and conveys an expectation that someone else do something about the unfair state of your life. It's a good way to stay immobilized, complaining about what *should* be rather than accepting what is and working to change it if you want something different.

"It's not fair" language fixes blame rather than fixes the problem. It helps you deny responsibility for searching for a solution and keeps you stuck in the right/wrong aspect of the situation. Creating a more workable balance of conflicting interests in your life happens best when you drop "fair" from your Couple Talk repertoire and focus instead on the language of solution-seeking.

The language of solution-seeking focuses on the sharing of feelings, desires, and prejudices. A proper balance in conflicting interests rarely occurs without addressing the individual feelings and desires behind the perceived imbalance. Balance is found through the open discussion of emotions and attitudes that surround the behavior that is considered "unfair."

Instead of saying, "I always have to get up with the kids. It's not fair," drop the reference to fairness and ask for what you want. Tell your partner, "I'd like to sleep through the night. I'd like you to get up with the kids." Be honest, open, and specific in your request.

Change "You seem to have time for your hobby. It's only fair that I get time for mine" to "I'd like a couple of hours to engage in my hobby this weekend. Will you support me in that?" Or talk about your feelings as detailed in Chapter 2; for example, "I'm feeling frustrated that my hobby is being neglected." Still another Couple Talk choice is to use a phrase explained earlier in this chapter. Invite your partner to do some problem-solving with you by asking, "How can we both get what we want?"

It may seem to you as if we're saying, Life is not fair; get over it. A more accurate assessment of our view is, Life is not fair; do something about it. The tools for doing something about it are in this chapter and spread throughout the book. When you perceive inequities in your relationship, you can address that imbalance by using language that builds mutual respect, caring, and intimacy. That can be done best when you drop "It's not fair" language from your Couple Talk.

HEARING

When you hear, "It's not fair," listen carefully for the perceived imbalance in the behavior your partner is drawing your attention to. Turn down the volume on the fair/unfair reference and turn up the volume on the underlying issue. Concentrate on your partner's feelings and attitudes about what is occurring. Move the discussion beyond the issue of fairness and into the area of seeking appropriate balance in your relationship.

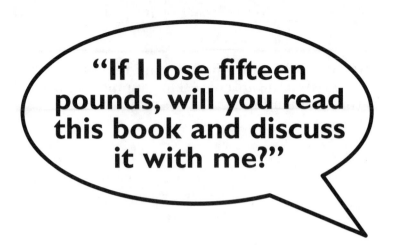

"If I lose fifteen pounds, will you read this book and discuss it with me?"

During solution-seeking, stalemate sometimes occurs. These are situations where neither partner wants to budge from their stated position. A mutually agreeable solution to the problem seems out of reach. In these cases we recommend the *contingent action proposal*.

A contingent action proposal is a way of offering your partner a deal. In essence, it says, If I do this, will you do that? or If you do this, I will do that. It's an attempt to break a deadlock by creating a trade-off that both parties will accept.

Examples include:

"If we go to your mother's this weekend, will you agree to leave Sunday morning?"

"If I prepare Thanksgiving dinner for your family, will you accept a stay-at-home Christmas day?"

"If you're willing to let me plan the next vacation, I'll agree to do the horseback riding adventure in Montana."

"If we all go for a family portrait, will you agree to stick with the basic package they offer and not order extras?"

"If I consent and tell you my hottest sexual fantasy, will you agree that it will never be talked about outside of our bedroom?"

"If you're willing to assume total responsibility for feeding and cleaning up messes in the yard, I'll agree to get a dog."

If solution-seeking is going nowhere, if you seem to be spinning your wheels, consider using Couple Talk that offers a contingent action proposal. It might be the strategy that propels you toward consensus and mutual respect.

HEARING

When you hear your partner offer an "if/then" deal, know that they are attempting to break the stalemate. Understand that they are searching for a way to end the disagreement with a solution that is acceptable to both of you. Seriously consider the offer. If you can accept it, fine. If not, say that, and offer a contingent action proposal of your own.

True or false?

1. People who have great relationships never fight.

2. Arguing is a sign that the honeymoon period is over.

3. The number of times that couples argue affects the stability of their relationship.

4. Fights signal structural weakness in a relationship.

IF YOU MARKED ANY of the above statements *true*, you're in for a surprise. We believe the answer to each item is false.

Arguments are not positive or negative. Fights are not necessarily good or bad. In reality, the value or harm associated with a fight depends on *how* you fight. Let's take a closer look.

If you fight fair, following agreed-upon rules, fighting has several relationship benefits. Fighting releases pressure. It serves as a safety valve to keep tension at a manageable level. It creates trust in the relationship because your partner knows you are not seething inwardly, refusing to acknowledge or express your concerns. He or she also learns over time that you will not humiliate or ridicule them for arguing about the issues they consider important.

Conflict avoidance, suppression of feelings, and denial of issues generate relationship challenges that are just as serious as those created by verbal confrontations. Pushing down and numbing out anger, resentment, and irritation does not create healthy relationships. Those feelings have to go somewhere. They have to surface sooner or later. Often, they come out attached to unrelated issues, causing confusion, misunderstanding, and hurt feelings.

If you use Couple Talk that attacks character or ridicules personality, you are not fighting fairly. Stay away from abusive language and name-calling. Do not beat up your partner with excessive dialogue and broken-record statements. Refrain from a win-at-all-costs approach that robs your partner of his or her dignity. To be nondestructive in your fighting, observe some basic rules: Take turns. Check for understanding. Call a time-out if necessary. Stick to the issue at hand. Own your feelings. And keep the issue in perspective.

Arguments are not something to look forward to or schedule on a regular basis. You should not attempt to create them. On the other hand, do not allow them to intimidate you. If they happen, they happen. It's unlikely that two people with physical, emotional, spiritual, and psychological differences would never disagree. Going eyeball to eyeball with the one you love is normal. Accept it and use it as an opportunity to strengthen your relationship.

HEARING

If you hear what sounds like the beginning of a fight, don't panic. Check it out. Inquire, "Are we going to fight about this?" If the answer is affirmative, your partner is telling you something. He or she is saying that this issue is so important to them and their feelings are so strong about it that they want to do battle.

It's OK to fight back as long as you fight fairly. Mix listening with the explanations of your thoughts, ideas, and feelings.

Appreciate your partner for fighting rather than running. Value them for arguing rather than stonewalling. Acknowledge the high energy state an argument generates and think about how much better it is than the low energy state of depression or pouting.

Later, debrief the argument. Suggest, "Let's talk about how we fought."

CHAPTER 5

The Language
of Respect

FIFTEEN THINGS TO SAY
TO SHARE APPRECIATION

1. "Thank you for _____."

2. "I appreciate it that _____."

3. "I'm feeling really loved right now."

4. "There is no way I could have done this without you. Thanks."

5. "I really wanted your help. Thanks for being there for me."

6. "You really helped me when _____."

7. "Your effort with _____ made things a lot easier for me."

8. "I was so happy to see _____. Now I have time to _____."

9. "If it wasn't for you, I wouldn't have been able to _____."

10. "That put a spring in my step and a smile on my face."

11. "Let me give you a big hug."

12. "It's so much fun to be loved by you."

13. "You never cease to amaze me. Thank you for _____."

14. "What a positive model you are for me!"

15. "I feel so blessed to have you here."

"You could be right about that."

"I don't think so, but you might be correct."

"Could be."

"There is a chance you could be right."

"Your answer is one possibility."

"I definitely disagree, and your way could be the right one."

THERE ARE OCCASIONS when you absolutely know you are right. You know that you're supposed to turn north and your partner thinks you should turn south. You know the White Sox played the Dodgers in the 1957 World Series and your wife thinks it was the Yankees vs. the Dodgers. You know the vacation is only going to cost fifteen hundred dollars and your partner thinks it will cost double that figure.

It is at times like these that it's important to keep in mind the adage, *Being right doesn't work.* Being right or acting as if you are right creates emotional separation and puts distance between you and your partner. Comments like "You're wrong about that," "No way,"

"That's impossible," "You're mistaken," and "You can't be right" not only make you right, they make your partner wrong. When you make your partner wrong, you don't build goodwill, connectedness, or happy relationships.

The pleasure of being right doesn't compensate for the ill feelings generated by making your partner wrong. So even when you are one hundred percent sure of your correctness, we suggest you use a variation of the phrase, "You could be right about that."

"You could be right, but I think we went left the last time we visited them" allows for the possibility that your partner could be correct. It shows respect for their opinion even if you don't agree with it. In addition, it could prevent you from getting egg on your face in the event you turn out to be incorrect.

"I suppose it could have been the Yankees and the Dodgers, although I'm pretty sure I remember Ted Kluszewski hitting two home runs for the Sox in game one" allows your partner to save face when she eventually finds out that Early Wynn was the winning pitcher for the White Sox that day. Using the Couple Talk phrase, "It could have been," communicates a basic respect for your partner. Including "pretty sure" allows for the possibility that what your partner thinks is true.

"You could be right about that" comes across as less rigid. It positions you as a person who can keep an open mind and consider other possibilities, even when you know that you're correct. That's how you'd like to be treated by your partner and that's how your partner wants to be treated by you.

You may be thinking that you and your partner like to argue and enjoy proving each other wrong. You might feel it is energizing and does absolutely no damage to your relationship. We don't think so, but you could be right about that.

HEARING

When you hear the phrase, "You could be right about that," know that your partner has respect for your opinion. Do not interpret the phrase as agreement. Do not hear that he or she thinks you are correct. Hear that they still believe firmly in their position but honor your idea as a possibility.

"You were
right about that."

"I was wrong."

"I learned something from you on this one."

"I made a mistake."

"I was way off base this time."

"You were absolutely correct."

"You were right about that" is Couple Talk that signals your partner can own up to his or her mistakes. It communicates a willingness to admit an error and acknowledge the learning that took place. It demonstrates maturity and reflects a controlled ego that is not afraid to learn and grow.

When Rachael realized that her effort to help her brother fell on deaf ears, she told her husband, "You were right on target about that situation."

After attending his first English class at a local university, Pablo shared his positive experience with his wife by saying, "You were correct. I will be able to handle this class."

After checking the Internet to find the closest star to the earth, Brandon admitted, "I found the information on the star today. I was off base. I learned something from you on this one."

While admitting you were wrong is important in a mutually respectful partnership, it does not require putting yourself down in the process. "I sure was wrong about him. Was I ever stupid!" is self-deprecatory. "I sure was wrong about him" is sufficient. "Was I ever stupid!" is unnecessary. "I was way off base on that one. I don't know how you live with a low I.Q. person like me" includes information that is not needed. Eliminate the put-down concerning your I.Q. and let the "off base" admission stand by itself.

If you are wrong, admit it. Acknowledge your error and move on. Nothing else is needed.

HEARING

When you hear your partner admitting a mistake, know that you have hooked up with a mature person. Hear more than their words of admission. Hear a desire on their part to set the record straight. Hear an absence of a need to be right. Hear the maturity of an ego that can handle imperfection. Hear the respect and appreciation that flows from your partner to you.

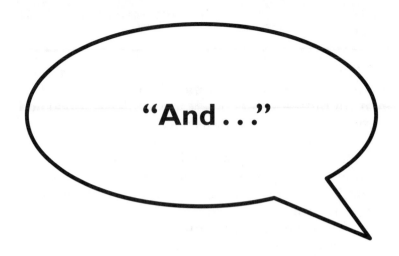

"And . . ."

"I liked the place you chose for dinner, but . . ."

"You look handsome tonight, but . . ."

"That sounds like fun, but . . ."

"BUT" IS A SMALL but extremely powerful word. It appears harmless enough at first glance—a conjunction used to connect or contrast two parts of a sentence. Its function is to separate ideas, dividing and creating distance between what comes before it and what comes after it.

Used often and carelessly, "but" can also create separateness in your relationship.

When the word "but" is used, it is often heard in a way that puts a negative connotation on the statement that preceded it. "You look good in that outfit, but I like the other one" can be heard as, I'm not really sure about that outfit. "I hear you, but I'm not in complete agreement" can be heard as, I'm not fully listening to you.

In some cases the word "but" focuses our attention on what follows and completely negates the intent of the previous statement. "I like the way you did that, but I would do it this way" gets interpreted as, I don't really like the way you did that. "I want to stay home with the kids, but I need to go to work" can be heard as, I don't want to stay home with the kids.

What do you hear in the statement below?

"I have a person that would be a great employee for your company. She is punctual, good with people, energetic, and has a positive outlook, but she sometimes has a problem managing her anger."

Was your attention drawn to the problem with anger? Did you focus more on anger management than on punctuality, energy, or positive outlook? Consider how the word "but" affected what you heard and felt about this potential employee.

"But" dismisses what came before it. It announces that what follows is the important part of the communication. It signals the listener to ignore what came previously because the really important stuff is about to be delivered.

A small adjustment in your Couple Talk can make a huge difference in how your words are being heard and interpreted. To help your partner hear what you intend, replace "but" with "and." By simply changing one word you will help your partner hear you more accurately and understand your intent more directly. Consider these examples:

"I like the way you did that, and I
would do it this way."

"I love you, and I don't like it when you do that."

"You look good in that outfit, and I like
the other one better."

Hear the difference? "And" is a word that combines ideas rather that separates them. It pushes ideas together rather than pulls them apart. "And" joins the two parts of the sentence, giving them equal importance. It helps us hear and see the whole picture rather than concentrating on the limiting components.

HEARING

When you hear your partner use the word "but," mentally change it to the word "and." Give both parts of the sentence your attention and consideration. Strive to hear all of what was included, both before and after the "and." Our guess is that you will be amazed at the results. *And* then again, maybe you won't. Guess you'll have to see for yourself.

"I can see that you're angry."

"It sounds like you're struggling to put
your feelings into words."

"We need to talk about this."

"I know when you're upset. And this is
one of those times."

THESE STATEMENTS SEEM INNOCENT enough at first
glance. Yet, if your partner is caught in the grips of
strong emotion, their use may be similar to lighting
the fuse on a stick of dynamite.

When you notice something that you would like to
point out to your partner, we suggest you begin with
the phrase, "It seems to me . . ." This piece of Couple
Talk tends to soften the edge and make what you have
to say easier for your partner to hear.

"It seems to me" is a simple adjustment that can
make a huge difference in how the message is heard.
Simply add the phrase to what you were already about
to say. "I can see that you're angry" becomes "It seems
to me that you're angry." "We need to talk about this"

turns into "It seems to me that we need to talk about this." "It seems to me that you're upset" replaces "I can see that you're upset."

"It seems to me" is Couple Talk that is less confrontational and sounds gentler to the ears of the receiver. Without that qualifying phrase, your words tend to be interpreted as a factual statement, producing the potential for defensiveness. "It seems to me that something is wrong" does not say that something *is* wrong, only that it *seems* to be that way. There is still room for discussion and disagreement.

It seems to us that this phrase is subtle, but important. It seems to us that it could work to strengthen your Couple Talk. It seems to us that when you use this phrase, you will be amazed.

HEARING

"It seems to me . . ." is a verbal communication that your partner has some information they wish to share in as gentle a way as possible. The use of this phrase is a sign that he or she realizes that what they are about to say is based on their own point of view and they wish to check it out with you. You are being presented with your partner's interpretation of what is happening.

"It seems to me" is a subtle way of opening a discussion around what could be a hot topic. Resist being defensive. Hear your partner's language choice as one made out of respect for you and your point of view.

"Thank you."

NOTICE THAT THIS COUPLE TALK PHRASE consists of only two words. It is not "Thank you for taking out the garbage," or "Thank you for giving me the support and encouragement I needed." It is simply "Thank you." End of sentence.

While noticing and thanking your partner for their efforts or energy is important and worthwhile, it is not what this "thank you" message is about. "Thank you" in this context is a phrase we suggest you use in direct response to a compliment.

"You look handsome tonight."

"Thank you."

"I was proud to be with you tonight."

"Thank you."

"You were the prettiest girl at the dance."

"Thank you."

"That was a good question."

"Thank you."

Responding to compliments with a simple "Thank you" will prevent you from denying, disowning, or discounting your partner's positive words. How often have you said, "You look great tonight," only to hear your spouse remark, "I need to lose fifteen pounds"? The discounting of compliments is a common occurrence in our society. We often respond to compliments as if we will appear too egotistical if we don't temper them with a degree of negativity. Consider the following compliments and responses.

"You look nice today."

"I can't seem to get my hair right."

"You were using your brain power on that."

"Anybody could have done the same thing."

"The car shines."

"I could have done better if I'd had more time."

A compliment is a statement of what your partner believes about you. When you respond to the compliment with a simple "Thank you," you are not agreeing or disagreeing with it. You are simply allowing it to exist in the universe without any need to alter it.

Let your partner's compliment in. Let it filter its way through your body, from the top of your head to the tip of your toes. Resist the urge to send it careering back to the sender with a discount. Just say, "Thank you."

Another valuable application of the "Thank you" phrase is as a response to an offhanded compliment.

"You really have a weird sense of humor."

"Thank you."

"You're a strange man."

"Thank you."

Saying "Thank you" to these thinly veiled put-downs tells your partner that what you just heard you intend to take as a compliment. It is a technique you can use to keep from taking offense at their words. It changes the focus of the communication by lightening up the situation with an unexpected reaction to the camouflaged put-down.

At this point you may be thinking, You guys are really far out on some of this stuff. Thank you.

Hearing

When your partner says "Thank you" following receipt of a compliment, know that it was heard and appreciated.

If you hear "Thank you" at what seems like an inappropriate time, you might want to examine the message you just sent. It could be that your communication was an offhanded put-down and your partner is attempting to deflect it without taking it personally.

BE CAREFUL how you use, "If it weren't for you." The words that you choose to complete this sentence starter will demonstrate or deny respect, build or destroy connectedness, and strengthen or weaken the communication process.

Use "If it weren't for you" to send a message of appreciation to your partner.

"If it weren't for you, our finances
would be a mess."

"If it weren't for you, I wouldn't know about
the new child seat belt laws."

"If it weren't for you, I would have trouble
finding time to write my book."

"We would be stuck in traffic right now
if it weren't for you."

"Our children wouldn't love to read as much
as they do if it weren't for you."

Adding an appreciative comment to your "If it weren't for you" message acknowledges your partner's efforts. These uplifting statements recognize his or her accomplishments and describe the impact they have on your life. They offer sincere appreciation for an important contribution your partner has made.

On the other hand, there is danger in using the Couple Talk phrase, "If it weren't for you," when you add a heavy-duty ending that places intense pressure on your partner to keep performing or suffer tragic consequences.

"If it weren't for you, I would commit suicide."

"If it weren't for you, life would be hell."

"I'd be nothing if it weren't for you."

"Our son would be in jail if it weren't for you."

"If it weren't for you, I would have no
peace of mind at all."

Using "If it weren't for you" in this way places too much responsibility on your partner. It is a way of disowning responsibility for your own life while communicating to your partner your expectation of continued rescuing, placing them in the position of having to continue their efforts or risk tragic results.

Some people use, "If it weren't for you," to assign blame.

"If it weren't for you, we'd have more
money to spend."

"I wouldn't be overweight if it weren't for you."

"If it weren't for you, the kids wouldn't
act this way."

"If it weren't for you, life would be a lot more fun."

> "I'd feel a lot better about myself
> if it weren't for you."

Used in this way, "If it weren't for you" becomes an attempt to deny ownership of the problem and absolve yourself of responsibility for dealing with it.

Pay attention to how you use, "If it weren't for you." Do you use it to place blame and deny ownership? ("If it weren't for you, we would have a nice home right now.") Do you use it to apply pressure and establish unrealistic expectations? ("If it weren't for you, life wouldn't be worth living.") Do you use it to acknowledge your partner's efforts and uplift their spirits? ("We wouldn't be able to go on a nice vacation like this if it weren't for you.")

HEARING

When you hear the phrase, "If it weren't for you," listen carefully to what follows and try to determine its intent. Is it meant to fix blame, apply pressure, or communicate sincere appreciation? If you feel pressure, say, "Not true," or "I don't believe that to be true." If you sense that blame is your partner's intention, ask, "What did I say/do that gave you that idea?" or say, "No, that is not true." When you hear sincere appreciation, acknowledge it with a simple "Thank you."

"I need to vent."

"I AM TOTALLY EXASPERATED! The grass needs mowing. This house is too small. Our friends are boring. So is our sex life. The dog dumps in the yard and no one cleans it up. Your mother expects me to talk to her for hours on the phone. I hate this. My life is awful." Ever walk into one of these buzz saws without seeing it coming? Wasn't fun, was it?

If you need to vent, we recommend you ask permission first. Warn your partner. Let them know that everything but the kitchen sink is on the way. "I'm having a terrible, no-good day and I need to vent. Are you up to it?" is a good way to inform your partner of the verbal storm that is about to be unleashed. It will help them to listen and witness the forthcoming deluge without taking it personally.

Sometimes we need to vent. Sometimes just getting it out helps us to refocus and move forward. Having a compassionate partner who can stand in the middle of our tirade and simply be there without commenting or judging is an incredible blessing. Treat that blessing with respect by warning your partner of the impending barrage of words and by asking his or her permission to use them as a verbal punching bag.

HEARING

If your partner is in control enough to warn you of their need to vent, be thankful. Often venting arrives without warning.

With or without a warning, hear the venting as frustration needing to be released into the universe. Consider it a cleansing process. Your partner is ridding himself or herself of negative, self-defeating emotions so that they can re-center and get back on track.

Know this is not who your partner really is. Know that it is not about you. You don't have to do anything. Being present is enough.

Eulice had been uncharacteristically judgmental and critical all weekend. His tone communicated irritation. His manner was abrupt and his demeanor distant.

On Sunday night, Eulice apologized to his partner, Lilly. He explained that a tight deadline at work was creating stress and worry for him. After acknowledging his rude behavior, he pledged to be different and said he was sorry.

Lilly took a moment to collect her thoughts before she responded. Then she told him, "Eulice, I didn't particularly care for the way you treated me this weekend and I know that is not who you really are."

With the words, "I know that is not who you really are," Lilly told her partner that she saw him as more than his immediate behavior. She saw beyond his current act and recognized the light and love that is his essence. Lilly held a larger view of Eulice than his recent behavior revealed, and she used effective Couple Talk to help him appreciate that.

Sometimes our partners forget who they really are. They temporarily lose sight of the love that exists within them. When this occurs it is important to communicate how we hold them in our consciousness, helping them appreciate that we see in them more than they are currently seeing in themselves.

"I know that is not who you really are" is not to be used as a shaming tactic. "You forgot your own son's birthday. That's not who you really are." It is not a strategy for communicating disappointment. "You promised to take us to the zoo and now you say you're too busy. Who you really are is not a person who disappoints his family." It is not a technique to dispense guilt. "You could be so much more than this. This isn't how you really are." It is not an attack weapon. "What's the matter with you? This isn't who you really are."

"I know that's not who you really are" is best communicated with a loving tone and an open heart. It is a gentle reminder to your partner of how you see them. It speaks to the innocence of their soul rather than to the guilt of their ego. It honors the love that exists even if it is not currently being shown.

HEARING

When your partner says, "I know that's not who you really are," hear that they see the real you, the one that is love and light. Realize that they see beyond your present act and recognize your true essence, even if you have temporarily forgotten it.

"Do you really want to know?"

"DO YOU REALLY WANT TO KNOW?" is a Couple Talk phrase to use when you are confronted with a difficult question and are uncertain about whether or not to answer it in a straightforward manner. It is both a courtesy check and a subtle way of warning your partner: If I answer honestly, I might say something that you won't like. Are you ready to hear it? Is that what you want?

Consider using the phrase when your partner asks a question where it seems that whatever answer you give is likely to result in an argument. Such questions include:

"Do you think I look better now that
I've lost weight?"

"Do you like my new hairstyle?"

"How much did you spend on that?"

"What time did you get home last night?"

"How many sexual partners did you
have before me?"

"Have you ever lied to me?"

"What did you buy your last girlfriend
for her birthday?"

"Did you do that with your first wife?"

Although these questions sound as if your partner
is seeking an honest, direct answer, how do you know
if it's a sincere request? To be sure, check it out before
you respond. Ask, "Do you really want to know?"

"Do you really want to know?" is not an effort to
sidestep the question. It is simply a way of offering
your partner the opportunity to consider whether he
or she really wants to hear your honest opinion. It
communicates: Are you ready for me to be open and
direct with you right now? I don't intend to avoid the
issue. I'm willing to tell you whatever you want to
know. I just want to be sure that you're ready.

This invitation to your partner to look within,
check out their feelings, and determine whether or
not they really want an answer gives them a chance to
withdraw the question or defer asking it to another
time. Withdrawing the question is not uncommon
when someone realizes that they are about to get a
straight answer. Sometimes they don't really want to
know—at least at that moment, although they may be
ready at another time.

Consider the Couple Talk examples that follow.
Notice how the conversation between Jodi and Steve
changes based on whether or not the phrase, "Do you
really want to know?" is used. First is a conversation
without its use.

Jodi: "Do you think I look better now that I've lost
weight?"
Steve: "Yes, I think you do."
Jodi: "Oh, so you didn't like the way I looked before."
Steve: "No, I didn't mean that."
Jodi: "Then what did you mean?"

Now consider the conversation that includes the phrase.

Jodi: "Do you think I look better now that I've lost weight?"

Steve: "Do you really want to know?"

Jodi: "I think I do, but I'm not sure what you'll say."

Steve: "How would what I say affect how you feel about yourself after losing the weight?"

Jodi: "I guess it really wouldn't matter, now that I think about it."

Steve: "So do you really want me to tell you what I think?"

Jodi: "Yes."

Steve: "I think you do look better and I hope you feel good about your accomplishment."

Jodi: "I do. Thanks."

The goal of asking, "Do you really want to know?" is to get truthful answers in the face of difficult questions. It does not give you permission to make a hurtful comment and then shrug it off with "Well, I asked you if you wanted to hear it and you said you did." Any answer you give should be expressed with love and caring.

Sometimes when you use this phrase your partner will *tell* you that they want to know, but their actions and words will indicate that they are not ready to hear the truth. Although they say, "Yes, I really want to know," they may react angrily and defensively. If you feel attacked, call a time-out. Say, "It doesn't seem as though you really want to talk about this right now. Would you rather talk about it at a different time, when you're in a better place?" This kind of comment serves two purposes. It acknowledges and confronts the anger/defensive response, and it allows your partner the space they need to explore and manage their feelings about the subject.

HEARING

"Do you really want to know?" is a signal that you are about to enter the truth-and-honesty-zone. Check to see if you are really ready to hear a straightforward, honest answer. If you aren't, say no. Or tell your partner, "Not at this time." You can come back to your question later, when you feel truly ready to hear an honest response.

"I have something to tell you. Are you ready to hear it?"

WHEN YOU HAVE some important information to give to your partner and you're uncertain about how it will be handled, begin with a statement that delivers a "heads up" message—a clue that important and sensitive information is to follow. "I have something to tell you" elicits your partner's attention. "Are you ready to hear it?" is the warning phase of the communication. Consider the case of Stacy and Roger.

Stacy was filled with guilt and worry. Six months earlier, about the same time she had begun dating Roger, her current boyfriend, she had slept with someone else. Since then, she had dated Roger exclusively. She wished she had never slept with the other guy and was worried that Roger would find out, become angry, and end their relationship.

Stacy felt stuck. If she didn't tell Roger herself, he might find out through the rumor mill, resulting in hurt feelings as a result of her deceit and cover-up. On the other hand, if she came right out and told him, he might still feel hurt and angry. Either way, she risked losing Roger and the meaningful relationship they had come to share.

In therapy, Stacy revealed to her therapist both what she had done and her desire to stay with Roger. She realized that she truly loved him, but if they were to stay together she knew she would have to tell him what had happened. She would also have to tell him how she felt about what she had done and how she felt about him. To assist her in the process, her therapist suggested the Couple Talk phrase, "I have something to tell you. Are you ready to hear it?"

"Roger, I have something to tell you," Stacy began the next time she and Roger were together. "It's something that has been bothering me. My heart hurts to hold it inside. I want to tell you, but I think what I have to say may hurt you."

"What it is?" Roger responded.

"Are you ready to hear it?" Stacy asked.

"Yes, I want to hear it," Roger assured her.

Hurt and anger did surface during the conversation that followed. But so did love and appreciation. Roger was given an opportunity to check inside and see if he was ready to handle a difficult topic. He had the choice of declining or accepting the invitation. He could have deferred it until later, but in this case he opted to move forward immediately and he effectively handled the choice he made.

HEARING

When your partner uses this phrase, be prepared to hear some sensitive, perhaps intimate, information that may challenge your relationship. He or she is prepared to take a huge step. It is a signal that they believe both you and the relationship are worth taking the risk of being honest, even though it may cause some pain.

Before you give a quick answer to this question, check inside to be sure that you're ready to hear whatever your partner has to say. Decide whether or not you are really ready to handle sensitive information. If the answer is yes, you will need to be ready to listen effectively and to manage whatever feelings arise with empathy and caring for your partner. A yes response will present you both with an opportunity to learn, grow, and stretch as individuals and as a couple.

If you are not ready to hear whatever information your partner presents, tell them no, or not at this time. You can always change your mind later.

CHAPTER 6

The Language of Disrespect

"You really lucked out."

MARY ELLEN COULD BE DESCRIBED as nonassertive. She tended to favor her quiet side and did little to attract attention to herself. That being the case, it came as a bit of a surprise when she found herself calling the president of the local Lions Club to request two thousand dollars.

Mary Ellen wanted the money for her fifth-grade students. It was only the first week in January and they had already read most of the books in their small school library. The middle school library was several miles away, and many of the books housed there were well beyond fifth-grade reading level. No community library existed.

The school principal claimed he had no money in his budget for books. The school board had just watched their request for a millage increase go down to defeat.

Caring deeply about her cause, Mary Ellen decided to push the situation by taking it to a new level. She prepared a list of the books she wanted, itemized the costs involved, created a budget, designed a needs statement, and wrote a page of rationale detailing why she wanted the money and how it would serve the children in the community.

With the planning phase behind her, Mary Ellen gave herself a quick pep talk, took a deep breath, and dialed the number of the Lions Club president. The call, her hard preparation work, and her verbal skills got her a place on the agenda at the next general meeting.

Two weeks later Mary Ellen took her cause to the Lions Club membership, made a formal presentation, and answered questions. After a vote by the members, she walked away from the meeting with a check in hand for two thousand dollars.

When Mary Ellen returned home she excitedly showed the check to her husband, Larry. The first words out of his mouth were, "You really lucked out there." Larry spent the rest of the evening trying to figure out why his wife had gotten so angry and attempting to get back on her good side.

When Larry said to Mary Ellen, "You really lucked out," she felt slighted. She was upset because he had failed to recognize and affirm the role she played in the positive response she had gotten from the Lions Club. It was not luck that produced the money for books. It was Mary Ellen's preparation, skills, commitment, persistence, and effort.

Larry did not intentionally insult his wife. He simply chose to use Couple Talk that included the language of luck. Our language is filled with words and phrases that attribute success to luck—or the lack of it.

"You sure were fortunate."

"What a charmed life you lead."

"You were in the right place at the right time."

"What an unfortunate string of events."

"Lady Luck didn't smile on you this time."

"I guess you're jinxed."

"What a wonderful coincidence."

Life appears, in one sense, to be an ongoing mixture of good breaks and bad breaks. Yet, in another sense, it is nothing more than good or poor preparation, an abundance of skills or a lack of them, a choice to see many alternatives or few. Opportunities come and opportunities go. How a person chooses to see those opportunities and the skills and preparation he or she brings to them have more to do with success than good fortune does.

By using the language of luck, Larry negated his wife's efforts. His verbal response disowned the role she played in creating the outcome. He gave credit for her success to some mysterious, outside force termed "luck."

Do you hear the language of luck in your Couple Talk? Do you notice yourself using the words "fortunate," "magic," "accidental," "coincidence," and "lucky"? If so, you are denying the cause-and-effect relationship that exists in the world. You are looking past the choices made by your partner and diminishing his or her sense of personal power.

Why not choose language that gives your spouse credit for having the good sense to be in the right place at the right time? How about using words that acknowledge the effort and energy he or she brought to the job hunt? Why not let your language reflect an appreciation of how your partner's thoughts, imagination, actions, and follow-through were instrumental in bringing about the results they got rather than attributing their success simply to "luck" or "good fortune"?

HEARING

When your partner uses the words "luck," "fortunate," and "coincidence," he is embellishing the myth that luck exists and is at work in our lives. He is reinforcing his belief that he is not in control of the life situations that surround him. He is telling you that he is more comfortable giving credit or blame to some unknown, external force than to personal effort, energy, preparation, and skills.

Hear his language of luck as a statement of personal belief rather than as an attack on you. Refuse to take it personally. His language says more about him than it does about you. He is not intentionally putting you down. He simply does not have the same beliefs you do about the relationship between cause and effect and the issue of personal responsibility.

This is not a time to give your partner a lecture about luck or to assume your beliefs are superior to his. Opposite beliefs can exist in the same relationship if partners love and respect one another.

"This is the third time this week you've
been late for dinner."

"That's two years in a row you
forgot my birthday."

"I've had to tell you this three different times."

"You've got two strikes. One more
and you're out."

"That's three. Three times you've interrupted
me in the middle of this story."

THIS KIND OF COUPLE TALK indicates mental score-keeping. Keeping score mentally and announcing it verbally builds stress, magnifies the situation, and interferes with the process of communicating clearly and directly. When you keep track of the number of times a negative behavior has occurred, you're practicing a kind of archeological aggression—taking garbage from the past and dragging it into the present to be used as a weapon. The weight of numerous incidents creates strain and prevents you from dealing cleanly with the situation at hand.

Have you ever noticed how mental scorekeeping rarely occurs with positive behaviors? We seldom hear, "That's the fifth time this year you've brought me flowers," or "That's the sixth time this month you've told me how much you appreciate me." The reason we use mental scorekeeping only for negative behaviors is that it's a valuable tool for making our partner wrong. It supplies the proof we need to show that we are right. To step out of the role of scorekeeper, choose Couple Talk that treats each situation as new and different. Ask as if you have never asked before. Remind as if you had not reminded previously. Share your concern as if this is the first time you have ever shared it.

"John, would you please pick up your clothes?" is more effective than "John, I have asked you every day this week to pick up your clothes." "Please talk to me in a normal volume" has a greater chance of being heard than "That's the third time you yelled at me tonight." "Her phone number is 643-5059" shows more respect than "I've had to give you her number three times."

Putting a number on the frequency of the behavior and announcing it drags the past into the present, which can then be easily projected into the future, setting up a self-fulfilling prophecy. Monitor your Couple Talk. Listen for examples of mental scorekeeping. When you hear yourself verbalize a number, STOP. Dump the historical burden and deliver an honest and clear Couple Talk interaction that concentrates on the present.

HEARING

When your partner's communication includes a number, choose not to focus on the pattern. Do not debate the accuracy of the number or what it means about your character. Hear that your partner is concerned about the present incident, and craft your response to deal with that. If you can bring a caring resolution to the present incident, the importance of the number will fade along with the concern.

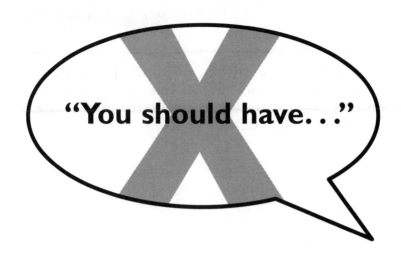

"You should have listened to me."

"You should have minded your own business."

"You should have bought the truck."

"You should have called him right away."

"You should have told me sooner."

"You should have asked me."

"You should have paid closer attention."

"You should have saved the money."

"You should have thought of that earlier."

"You should have listened to your mother
and married someone else."

IT IS ALMOST ALWAYS POSSIBLE to make a strong case
that your partner should have done something—or
done something different—in a particular situation.
So what? There is no point in laying blame for what

"should have" been done but wasn't. The useful question is not whether the "right" thing was done but what action is appropriate given the current situation. "Should have" is an effort to attach shame and fix blame. This phrase is designed to dispense guilt. Shaming, blaming, and guilt-tripping do not build positive relationships or leave your partner in an appropriate mood to begin the search for solutions.

A "should have" statement is a verbal grenade that blows up in the face of the person to whom it is delivered. In the explosion both parties get hit with shrapnel. You will create more positive results if you drop this verbal weapon from your language patterns rather than in the lap of your partner.

HEARING

When your partner tells you that you "should have" done something, hear it as data. Think of it as information they are sharing about their preferences. Consider it if you wish. Think about changing your response in the future if you choose.

Resist buying in to guilt. Think in terms of "could have" rather than "should have." It's true that you could have bought the truck rather than the car. You could have called your mother rather than choosing not to. And you could have taken your partner's advice rather than deciding on a different course of action. Certainly, you *could* have. But *should* you have? That's up to you.

"That's true, but . . ."

"I know, but . . ."

"OK, but . . ."

WANT TO HELP your mate feel wrong? Want them to come to the conclusion that everything they say is unacceptable? Then use the "Yes, but" response frequently.

Some people habitually use a "Yes, but" response in an attempt to balance a negative observation.

"We spent more money than we should have."

"Yes, but we got a really good deal."

"Our savings account is down to nothing."

"Yes, but we still have the stocks."

Other times the use of "Yes, but" is an unconscious attempt to cast the other in a bad light.

"You forgot to drop off the mail."

"Yes, but you don't remember half the things I tell you."

"Yes, but" is also used as a defensive response to a perceived accusation.

"You were paying a lot of attention to
Mary last night."

"Yes, but she needed some advice about her teenager."

A continuous stream of "Yes, buts" encourages the fight or flight response. Fight responses are characterized by defensiveness.

"You think you know everything. Well, you don't."

"Why don't you just shut up and listen for a while?
I get sick of hearing the sound of your voice."

"What makes you the expert?"

Flight responses are characterized by withdrawal.

Silence.

Sulking.

Pouting.

Self-talk: "There's no use in talking to her."
"I give up. He's impossible."

If you hear yourself using "Yes, but" frequently, stop and ask yourself: Is it more important to counter my partner's point right now or to help them feel understood? Is it more important to get my point across at this moment or to understand how my partner feels? If you decide that understanding your partner is the more important goal, summarize in words what you think you have heard so far. Paraphrase what you think he or she is saying and feeling. Summarizing and paraphrasing validate your partner and help them feel appreciated.

Summarizing what you think you heard does not necessarily mean that you agree with what you heard. It is an attempt to make sure you understood what has been communicated so far before the conversation moves on. Paraphrasing your partner's words or feelings doesn't mean theirs are correct and yours are wrong. What it does mean is that you hold the view that different ideas and feelings can coexist concerning the same topic. It communicates to your partner that you're open to the possibility that from their frame of reference, from where they stand, from their perspective, their conclusions may make sense.

As you read the last paragraph, did you form a "Yes, but" response in your head? If you did, consider it a clue that you may also be doing that with your partner. Ask yourself: Is it more important for me to be right about this paragraph or to understand what it says? If your goal is to understand, reread the paragraph without adding the "Yes, but."

Pay attention to your communication patterns this week. Be on the alert for "Yes, buts." If you hear yourself using or thinking that phrase, practice paraphrasing and summarizing instead. See how that works in your relationships.

HEARING

"Yes, but" could signal an honest attempt by your partner to balance the issue under discussion or it could be a tactic for proving his or her correctness. If you suspect clarification is your partner's intention, hear the word "and" in place of "but." "Yes, that's true, *and* . . ." creates the sense of adding a point to the discussion. "Yes, but" negates all that came before it and attempts to position what follows it as correct.

If "Yes, but" seems to be delivered in the spirit of proving rightness, stop the interaction and ask your partner if this is a discussion or an exercise to prove who is right. Invite them to participate in a discussion where ideas from both sides are heard and valued. Agree together to play with using "Yes, *and*" to replace "Yes, but."

"I was just kidding."

"I didn't really mean it."

"You know I wasn't serious."

"It was just a joke."

"Can't you take a little teasing?"

A USEFUL RULE OF THUMB regarding this kind of Couple Talk is: *If you don't mean it, don't say it.* Calling names, making fun of your partner, and teasing have no place in a loving relationship. Your role as a partner is to love, nurture, and support your beloved, not to be cute and clever with put-downs disguised as humor.

Humorous put-downs are seldom funny to the recipient. The person on the receiving end knows there is a hidden truth embedded in the communication. It's an attempt by the sender to deliver a put-down in a way that deflects personal responsibility by claiming they were only being funny. It's a way to be hurtful with a built-in out.

If you have something you want to communicate to your partner about his weight, tell him directly. If you think it's important to make a point about the age showing on your partner's face, send a clear message. If you want to remind your partner that her present behavior is incongruent with what she told her children yesterday, do it without joking. If you don't feel you can tell the truth, keep quiet.

Eliminate teasing and humorous put-downs from your Couple Talk. Instead, concentrate on your main responsibility: providing a safe harbor where love, support, and encouragement predominate.

HEARING

"I was only teasing" is an effort by your partner to duck responsibility for sending a hurtful message. Understand that he or she has some criticism of you that they didn't know how to communicate skillfully without wrapping it in humor to make it sound acceptable.

When you hear, "I was only teasing," reply, "I respond best to feedback when it comes without teasing. Could you please tell me another way?" This style of Couple Talk invites your partner to deliver the real message free of humorous content.

"I AM BETTY FRANK, AND THIS IS MY
HUSBAND, BRUTALLY."

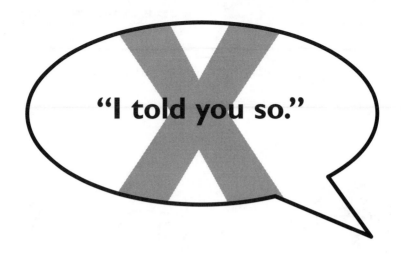

FORGET THIS PHRASE. Delete it from your Couple Talk file. Add it to that ever-increasing list of ways you used to talk before you knew better.

"I told you so" is nonproductive and divisive. It builds resentment. Your relationship does not need the emotionality, irritation, and distance that this phrase generates.

Carlos pulled his car into the parking structure and found an empty space. His girlfriend, Juanita, informed him, "If you park here you'll get a ticket." She pointed to a No Parking sign that could be interpreted as referring either to the space Carlos had his eye on or to the one next to it. In spite of Juanita's warning, Carlos chose to leave his car in the space in question.

Later, after a romantic dinner and dancing, the couple returned to the car hand in hand to find a ticket securely fastened to the windshield. "I told you so," Juanita said. Carlos said nothing, choosing to give Juanita the silent treatment.

Stewing over his girlfriend's pronouncement of her rightness, Carlos's resentment grew. So did his anger, which he pushed down and left unacknowledged. An evening that had begun filled with romance and tenderness ended with bitterness, confusion, and hurt feelings.

When Carlos found the ticket on his car, he didn't need anyone to point out to him who was right about the parking space. That was obvious. He was already feeling bad about having to pay a parking fine, and Juanita's "I told you so" not only aggravated the situation but turned his attention outward to the person he felt was rubbing it in rather than inward to the person who had made the decision about where to park the car.

Carlos's girlfriend would have been wise to hold her tongue in this situation. Empathy is what was needed, not a declaration of rightness.

"Bummer," "That's too bad," or "What a shame" are phrases that convey empathy. This style of communication says: I understand that you feel bad about this. Your feelings are more important to me than my need to be right.

Are you an "I told you so" person? If so, you may wish to consider the effect that style of language has on others. Is what you get from being right and drawing attention to it worth the price you pay? Does it serve your relationship and move it in the direction you desire?

In situations where you're tempted to say, "I told you so," bite your tongue. If you must, you can smile inwardly to yourself and have a private moment of satisfaction, but that's it. Keep the declaration of your correctness inside. Concentrate instead on sending love and caring in the direction of your partner. Include empathy and encouragement.

When you see evidence of the positive effects of your altered Couple Talk, remember where you read this. And know that, somewhere, both of us are smiling, biting our tongues, and thinking to ourselves: We told you so.

HEARING

If your partner says, "I told you so," you have a choice. You can take it personally and hear it as a declaration of rightness and an effort to rub in the fact that you were wrong, or you can hear that he or she is feeling small and weak and needs to bolster their sagging self-esteem. How you choose to hear their reaction will affect your response.

If you hear "I told you so" as rubbing it in, you will likely become defensive, take it personally, and activate a power struggle. You will want to get even and pay your partner back. You may blame him or her for your personal response, choosing to believe that their action is what caused your reaction.

On the other hand, if you hear "I told you so" as a signal that your partner is feeling low or needs to put you down so they can feel "better than," you will likely make a different response. You might joke about your poor choice, affirm your partner's abilities, or say simply, "This is another time when I wish I had listened to you." You won't allow their comment and a defensive response to spoil your evening.

Remember, your partner is in control of how a message is sent. *You* are in charge of how it is received. Whether you choose to hear, "I told you so," as an attack on you or as a signal of your partner's low self-esteem is up to you. It's your choice.

"Why won't you?"

JUDY HAD NOT BEEN SATISFIED in bed for several months. Her sexual encounters with her partner, Bob, had become boring and monotonous. In an effort to spice up her sex life, Judy asked Bob to try a different sexual position. He declined, stating, "No, I'm not comfortable with that."

Judy was hurt and mystified at her husband's reaction. She didn't understand his reluctance, so she asked him, "What bothers you about trying a new sexual position with me?" The question triggered a thirty-minute conversation that shed light on the situation. During the frank discussion, Bob told her of a past experience of sexual abuse of which Judy had no previous knowledge. One result of the sharing that occurred that night was a decision to work jointly with a sex therapist. That in turn led to increasingly enriched sexual experiences where both parties felt safe and comfortable.

Judy's asking "What bothers you?" initiated a productive dialogue with her husband. In phrasing the question that way, she successfully avoided one of the Couple Talk danger signals: the WHY question.

"Why won't you?" "Why did you?" "Why will you?" and similar questions put your partner on the defensive. "Why" questions sound as if an interrogation is about to begin. They are often perceived as an attack. They elicit answers that tend to terminate conversation. "What" questions more often serve to expand the conversation. They are perceived as seeking information. They communicate respect and caring.

Examine the following pairs of questions. Which question in each pair do you think invites increased discussion?

"Why won't you go to a therapist with me?"

"What worries you about going to a therapist with me?"

"Why can't you support me in this?"

"What are some of your concerns about supporting me in this?"

"Why can't you stop doing that?"

"What is it that keeps you from stopping that?"

"Why aren't you comfortable with that?"

"What could we change to help you feel comfortable with that?"

In our experience, "what" questions create more useful dialogue than "why" questions. "What" questions invite openness and build intimacy.

HEARING

When you hear a "why" question, resist the temptation to become defensive. Your partner is attempting to respect your relationship while getting information they feel is important. They are offering an invitation to expand the conversation. He or she wants dialogue and is trying to demonstrate respect and caring in an attempt to promote intimacy.

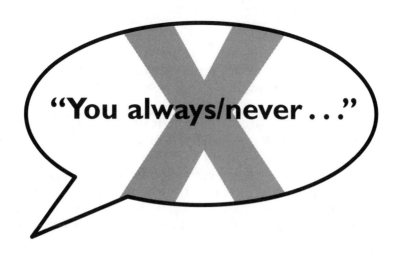

"You always/never..."

PAY CLOSE ATTENTION to how you use "always" and "never" with your partner. Used indiscriminately, these words can communicate negative expectations and sound accusatory.

"You never talk to me."

"You always spend too much money."

"We never go out to eat anymore."

"You always have trouble balancing
the checkbook."

"Why do you always interrupt me?"

An always/never attack invites defensiveness. Since exceptions to any accusation can be found, it is easy to deny the always/never message.

"I don't always have trouble balancing the
checkbook. I remember one time five years ago that
it came out accurately the first time I did it."

> "What do you mean I never talk to you? I talked to
> you the day before yesterday."

A person in the midst of denial is not able to attend to the present situation or to the specific circumstance that prompted the always/never comment in the first place. Furthermore, always/never is usually not true. There was a time when your partner did not spend too much money. She really doesn't interrupt you every time. Of course she talks to you sometimes. Doesn't she?

Eliminate "always/never" statements from your verbal feedback. Focus instead on what you want. Communicate that desire with an "I" statement.

> "I would like you to listen to me tonight."

> "I want to go out to dinner some night this week."

> "I don't like it when the balance in the
> checkbook isn't accurate."

Even positively phrased "always/never" comments are suspect.

> "I can always count on you."

> "You never give up."

> "You always say nice things to me."

Sometimes your spouse does give up. Can you really count on them every time? Do they *always* say nice things to you? Probably not. Your spouse knows on some level that your "always/never" comment is not true.

To be more accurate in your Couple Talk and continue to communicate positive expectancy, we suggest you change "always/never" to "usually" and "most of the time."

"I can usually count on you to come through."

"Most of the time you just don't give up."

"You say nice things to me so often."

Now your Couple Talk is consistent with reality and will help your partner internalize the positive message you want to send.

Free your Couple Talk of sweeping generalizations when giving your partner feedback. Save "always" and "never" for those rare instances when they are accurate descriptors.

Hearing

Make an effort to hear beyond "always/never" statements. When your partner says you never talk to her, she knows you talk to her sometimes. Instead of getting hung up on her use of "always/never," hear her frustration. Hear the specific complaint she is unskillfully verbalizing.

When he asks, "Why do you always interrupt me?" hear, I don't like it when you interrupt me. When he says, "You're never home on time," hear, I get frustrated when you're late. I wish you would come home on time.

"I SAID IT WITH WORDS. I WANT TO
TAKE IT BACK WITH FLOWERS."

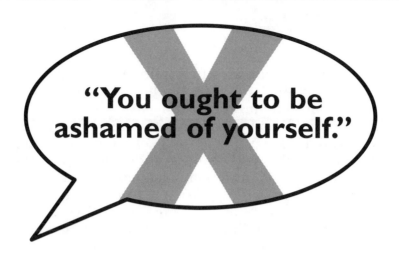

"You should have known better."

"You've really disappointed me this time."

"Your behavior is affecting my health."

"I can't sleep at night worrying about you."

A PARTNER USING THESE or similar phrases that communicate the message, "You ought to be ashamed of yourself," is playing the game of guilt-tripping. It's an attempt to get what he or she wants through manipulation and control. This kind of language reflects a belief that people must feel guilty before they will change—that if the other person can be shamed into feeling guilty, they will change their behavior and do what we want.

There are times when shaming works and produces the behavior we want from our partner. But at what price? Along with shame and guilt come the core beliefs, I'm not good enough; I'm wrong; I can never do anything right—not exactly the kind of beliefs we want to reinforce in our partner.

Shame and guilt are often counter-productive for another reason. The partner who is being shamed realizes on some level that they are being manipulated, pushed, and controlled. Manipulation breeds resentment. People who suspect they are being manipulated dig in their heels and resist outer control. Pushing is an invitation to be pushed back.

The alternative to selecting Couple Talk that attempts to shame is to communicate in a style that is open, honest, and direct. If you have strong feelings about a behavior or desired response, communicate it directly. Explain the reasons for your feelings. Be specific in your complaints. Tell how the behavior impacts your life.

Step away from the resistance-resentment cycle by telling your partner exactly what you prefer and why. "I want you to call me when you're going to be late so I don't worry" is more effective than "You should have known better." "I'm furious about this. Drinking and driving do not go together" is healthier than "You should be ashamed of yourself." "I would like you to stick up for me when your mother talks to me like that" is cleaner than "You've really disappointed me this time."

Shame and guilt are not congruent with a Couple Talk philosophy that focuses on mutual respect and honesty. Use the techniques presented throughout this book to replace language patterns that foster shame and guilt.

HEARING

If your partner is using shame and guilt to influence your behavior, hear more than unskillful communication. Hear beyond the shaming. Hear more than the guilt-tripping. Hear between the lines.

When you hear language that is an invitation to feel shame, ask yourself: What would he or she be saying if they could communicate their concern skillfully?

If your partner says, "You've really disappointed me this time," hear, I would like you to stick up for me when your mother talks to me like that. If she tells you, "You should be ashamed of yourself," hear the anger, worry, and frustration she feels when you combine drinking and driving.

If your partner is too emotionally caught up to express themselves skillfully, you still have the option of *hearing* skillfully. Separate the real issue from the guilt that you are being invited to feel. Respond only to the real issue.

"You slob."

"You're lazy."

"Idiot."

"You're bull-headed."

"You dumb blond."

"Jerk."

"Asshole."

"Bitch."

"Tramp."

"Bastard."

"Knucklehead."

IN LOVING RELATIONSHIPS, name-calling is not appropriate under any circumstances.

Name-calling is an attempt to inflict damage. It is an effort to wound the spirit. It is designed to produce pain.

Name-calling is not cute. It is not clever. It is not humorous.

Name-calling is verbal abuse. It is emotional violence—only one step removed from physical violence—and has no place in a respectful, caring partnership.

Name-calling creates feelings of separateness. It is divisive and invites resentment and retaliation.

If you or your partner moves into name-calling, stop immediately. Call a time-out. Go for a walk. Get away from each other for a while. Create some space and physical distance.

When you can talk without name-calling, use the skills presented throughout this book to communicate honestly and directly with each other. Talk about specific behaviors and feelings rather than inferences and judgments. Be descriptive and give behavioral examples. Listen until you are sure you understand what your partner is trying to communicate before speaking.

HEARING

If you are called a name, hear the anger underneath the insult and respond to the emotion rather than to the words with something like, "You must really be angry to talk to me like that. You sound furious and frustrated." Communicate your recognition of the emotional tension and refuse to add to it by retaliating with name-calling of your own.

TWENTY PHRASES THAT MAY INDICATE YOU HAVE AN ABUSIVE PARTNER

1. "Because I said so."

2. "It's your fault."

3. "I don't want you talking to/seeing her."

4. "I'll tell you what to do."

5. "You're not going out of the house looking like that."

6. "You don't need to know."

7. "I handle the money."

8. "You know what your problem is?"

9. "This is for your own good."

10. "You bitch!"

11. "Shut up!"

12. "You don't know what you're talking about."

13. "We're NOT doing it that way."

14. "If you don't like it, tough!"

15. "Get over it!"

16. "You'll be sorry."

17. "You'll never find anyone who will treat you as good as I do."

18. "We never [have sex/go on vacation/have any extra money/have any friends/have fun] because of you."

19. "I DARE you to [leave/find another man/lip off to me one more time/raise your voice to me]."

20. " . . . or else." "Don't you tell anyone, or else." "Get this house clean, or else." "Have my dinner ready when I get home, or else."

CHAPTER 7

The Language
of Boundaries

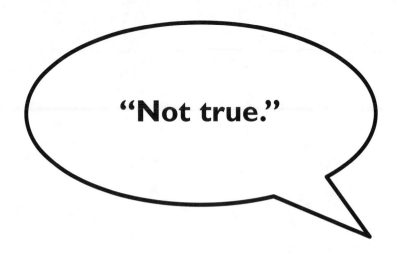

"Not true."

ANITA WAS IN THE MIDDLE OF EXPLAINING why she was frustrated at work. As she spoke, she noticed that her partner, Steve, wasn't totally focused on the conversation. It didn't take long for Anita to regain his attention when she angrily told him, "It's obvious you don't want to hear what I have to say."

"Not true," Steve replied. Then he added, "I do want to hear what you have to say. Your previous comment got me thinking about something else. I'm sorry I lost focus for a while. I'm still very much interested in hearing your concerns."

Anita correctly perceived Steve's momentary inattention. However, she did not know precisely what he was thinking in that instant. She made an assumption about Steve's thoughts and based her statement that Steve didn't want to hear what she had to say on that false assumption. Her conclusion was not true.

Notice that when Steve informed Anita that her statement was inaccurate, he did not say, "You're wrong." His words did not refer to his partner in any way. He did no finger-pointing. Instead, he used the Couple Talk phrase, "Not true," which spoke only to the accuracy of Anita's statement. He used, "Not true," to confront her conclusion and begin reframing Anita's interpretation of his behavior.

"Not true" is Couple Talk that tells your partner they have drawn an inaccurate conclusion and that their misinterpretation of your behavior will not go unchallenged. Some typical statements that could be answered with "Not true" and then reframed are:

"You don't love me anymore."

"You hate being around my parents."

"You're always thinking negative."

"You don't care."

"The children aren't important to you."

"I can tell that you're mad at me."

"You're afraid of me."

"You hate having to live on a budget."

"All you think about is sex."

"I know you're sorry you ever met me."

These statements can be correctly labeled "Not true" because they refer to your thoughts, your feelings, your perceptions, and your motivations. Your partner doesn't know whether or not you still love her. Only you do. He doesn't know if you care. Only you do. "Not true" is an appropriate response in these instances because the real answer, the accurate answer, is in your head or your heart.

Obviously, you only use "Not true" if the statement is untrue. Use "Not true" when you need to inform your partner quickly and cleanly that their assumption or inference is inaccurate. Use it when failure to challenge their statement would give the impression that it is, in fact, true. If your spouse tells you in the middle of an argument that you care more about the car than you do about her and you fail to respond, you send a signal that there is some truth to her statement. If your partner says, "I can't trust you anymore," and you

stand there and take it without dissent, you add cre-
dence to his accusation.

Even though your partner's inference is untrue, it
is important to listen well enough to understand more
clearly how they arrived at their conclusion. Balance
your desire to challenge an untrue statement with your
desire to listen for understanding by adding to your
"Not true" statement a request for further information
or clarification.

"Not true, but I'd like to hear why you think that."

"Not true, and I'd like to understand how you
could arrive at that conclusion."

"Not true, but keep talking. I'd like to hear more."

"I hear what you're saying and it's not true.
Please say some more."

"Not true. I do care. Tell me more."

"Not true. Tell me why you believe that."

"A lot of what you say is true. That last
statement is not true."

This style of Couple Talk will help you determine
if you have been doing or saying things that led your
partner to their conclusion. Be open to the possibility
that you could be influencing their assumptions.

HEARING

Hear "Not true" as an indication that your partner
disagrees with your previous statement. Stop and
think about what you just said. Check to see if you're
making an assumption about his or her feelings or
thoughts. Consider the possibility that your interpretation could be inaccurate.

Don't be threatened by this disagreement. See it as
an opportunity to explore differing perspectives and
to engage in a dialogue about how you're each demonstrating and perceiving feelings and thoughts.

"This is non-negotiable."

EVERYONE HAS A LIMIT to behavior they find acceptable. This limit is often called a "bottom line." Where your bottom line is drawn concerning a specific behavior depends on your level of tolerance for that behavior. Since tolerance levels are based on feelings, thoughts, and morals, you and your partner are likely to have a different tolerance level and a different bottom line on a variety of topics.

In building a respectful relationship, it's important to communicate limits. Respecting boundaries is difficult when boundaries are unclear or unspoken. Bottom lines that remain a secret create resentment, frustration, and misunderstanding. Articulating your bottom line is crucial to the respect of those boundaries.

"I will not tolerate hitting as a way to correct my children's behavior."

"Having sex with others is non-negotiable for me."

"Putting me down in front of other people is behavior that must end."

> "Telling ethnic jokes in my presence
> is unacceptable."

When you share what you will and will not tolerate, you define your personal space. You create a boundary. By sharing it with your partner you establish an area in which you expect a respectful response. These areas, by definition, are non-negotiable. These are behaviors about which you care so deeply that you're not willing to budge. Although flexibility may permeate much of your relationship, there is no flexibility here. This is your bottom line.

Your boundary or that of your partner can be about anything. Knowing how money is spent may be non-negotiable for you. Wearing a seat belt may be non-negotiable for your partner. A bottom line could be about cussing around the children, not smoking in the house, or who your partner spends time with after work. The line, based on your feelings and your comfort level, can be drawn anywhere, about any topic.

You and your partner will not be able to sit down and discuss every boundary and bottom line in advance. Often you won't know that you're nearing a bottom line until you get close to it. Therefore, it's important to agree to let each other know when a bottom line is being approached. Tell him or her, "You've bumped into one of those bottom-line issues for me. Let's talk about it later." Or say, "Honey, this is one of those non-negotiable behaviors for me."

HEARING

When you hear, "This is non-negotiable," your partner is letting you know that you've touched a bottom line. Hear how critical this issue is for them. Hear that this issue is so important that they have no room to negotiate. Be aware that you've reached a touchy area. Don't expect compromise. Don't expect flexibility.

Remember, this is not a preference. This is not a want. This is not a wish. This is a non-negotiable bottom line. If you hear the seriousness surrounding this issue, you'll have a greater chance of dealing with it successfully.

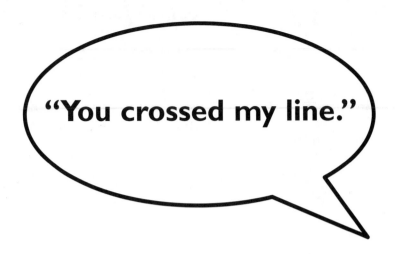

"You crossed my line."

MAIKO HAD A DISFIGURED LEFT FOOT. She was uncomfortable when others stared at it so she kept it hidden and told only her closest friends. She didn't like talking about it and quickly changed the subject if someone asked her about it.

When Maiko began dating Yoshi she was hesitant to show him her foot. She discussed it with him first and made it clear that the foot was a touchy subject. He promised to respect her feelings and desires about the deformity and asked to see it. Yoshi was surprised by the shape and look of the foot but treated Maiko and her desires with respect. She thought he understood.

Two months later Maiko was shocked to overhear Yoshi commenting to a friend, "You should see Maiko's foot. It really looks weird." She couldn't believe her ears. She was hurt and angry. She felt violated.

Later that night Maiko confronted Yoshi about his conversation with his friend. "What's the big deal?" he asked. "It's not that noticeable." Maiko informed him, "The big deal is not about my foot or what it looks like. The big deal is that I let you know that I'm supersensitive about my foot and you didn't respect that. I'm hurt and angry. You crossed my line. That's the big deal."

By using the Couple Talk phrase, "You crossed my line," Maiko made a clear statement of a boundary violation. She used it to let her partner know that he had violated a personal boundary. In doing so, she stood up for herself, stepped out of the victim role, and assumed a stance of empowerment. Although her words were, "You crossed my line," the real message she communicated was: I will not allow myself to be treated that way.

It took several serious discussions with Yoshi before Maiko felt he understood her position about her foot. It was difficult for her to continue to talk about it, yet she knew it needed to be done if she was going to get back to the position of feeling comfortable with Yoshi and seeing him as being respectful of her wishes and feelings.

Your personal boundary could be about your level of education or your weight. It could be about borrowing your clothes, calling you a particular name, or spanking the kids. It doesn't matter what your bottom line is about. It does matter whether or not it is respected.

Your partner will not know he or she crossed your line unless you tell them. We recommend you do that at least two times, before and after.

Talk to one another before boundaries are violated —not just about your likes and dislikes but about the limits that surround those likes and dislikes. By doing this you will prevent misunderstandings from occurring and establish clear boundaries that have a better chance of being respected. Then if a boundary is violated, "You crossed my line" becomes a subtle reminder of an earlier discussion.

When your partner knows ahead of time where your line is, they have a choice—a choice to respect it or ignore it.

When your articulated line is crossed, don't ignore it. To pretend it didn't happen or to let it go is to allow yourself to be victimized by your partner. Let your partner know, as Maiko did, that their choice crossed a personal boundary line. You cannot control what your partner says or does but you can control whether or not you let them know where your tolerance level is.

A boundary is based on one's moral and ethical position and on level of comfort. It's about personal thoughts and feelings. Defend your morals, your feelings, your thoughts. Protect yourself from being a victim of the behavior and words of your partner. Articulate your boundary line and inform your partner when he or she crosses it. Tell them, "You crossed my line."

HEARING

A boundary is meant to be respected, not ignored; honored, not broken; validated, not violated. When you hear your partner communicate that you have crossed their line, stop what you're doing or saying immediately. Back off and consider what you might have said or done that led to their feeling violated.

Avoid being defensive. Defensiveness only increases the feeling of being violated. Hear how important this is to your partner and stay open to hearing their side of the issue. If necessary, give them space. You can always return to the issue at another time. Later, seek to understand their feelings, thoughts, and morals before you attempt to present/defend your side of the issue.

Hear the respect your partner has for their own boundaries. Hear the way he or she stands up for him- or herself and refuses to be violated. Hear that your partner is a person of integrity who sets clear boundaries and communicates them with respect and caring.

"Back off."

"I NEED YOU TO BACK OFF right now." That's how Jack
informed his wife Heather that he wanted her to stop
pushing for an answer to her question about putting
their house up for sale. Heather was not offended. She
recognized the clue words, "Back off," from a Couple
Talk seminar they had attended months earlier. She
knew the "back off" signal meant Jack needed time,
space, and some distance from the situation. Hearing
that phrase reminded her that he was feeling pressured by her persistence and that further efforts to
persuade him would be fruitless. She backed off.

"Back off" is Couple Talk that asks your partner to
step aside or step back. It requests space and/or time.
It is a language technique intended to reestablish your
boundary line and reclaim your personal, physical, or
emotional space.

Other ways to say "back off" include:

"Please give me some space."

"I don't want to be close right now."

"You're moving in on me and it feels too tight."

"I'm feeling pressured by this and it's not helping."

"You're overwhelming me with your attention."

"I can't sort this out with you looking
over my shoulder."

"I need to get in touch with my own thoughts.
Please stop sharing yours right now."

Jack successfully implemented and Heather successfully responded to the "Back off" strategy because
they had talked about it beforehand. They had
defined together what "Back off" meant and how it
would be used. Their discussion of this Couple Talk
strategy included how far one was expected to back
off, what to do if the backing off wasn't far enough,
and how to reconnect when the backing off period was
over. They agreed that backing off when one of them
asked for it would be a way they could respect and
honor the other.

People often attempt to reclaim their personal
space and create distance with the phrase, "Leave me
alone." That phrase, accompanied by a negative tone,
can produce the result you asked for—loneliness.
"Leave me alone" is not recommended because it can
disconnect or separate you from your partner for
much longer than you desire. "Back off" can get you
the space and time you need without resulting in feelings of separateness.

A precautionary note: "Back off" messages need to
be balanced with "Come closer" messages. If you
exclusively send "Back off" messages, your partner
could begin to feel isolated and alone. Feelings of iso-
lation can create neediness, which draws your partner
closer in an attempt to reconnect. The resulting proximity behavior feels like hovering and generates the
opposite effect of what you requested with your original "Back off" plea.

"Back off" and its antithesis, "Come closer" (see "The Language of Intimacy" in Chapter 3), work in tandem. The more you use "Back off," the more you need to use "Come closer." The more you use "Come closer," the easier it will be to use "Back off." Each of these phrases requires the counterbalance provided by the other. Too much "Come closer" and you can feel smothered. Too much "Back off" and you create distance.

HEARING

The importance of this Couple Talk phrase lies not in what is said but rather in what is heard. When the phrase "Back Off!" reaches your ears, you have several possible choices. You can hear it as a personal slam. You can hear it as an invitation to do battle. You can hear it as the beginning of a power struggle. You can hear it as a threat or a warning. Or you can hear it as a signal that the person you love needs space.

You can also take a "Back off" request personally and interpret it as an affront to your caring. Or you can hear it as not being about you at all but as a statement about your partner and what his or her needs are at this moment.

Remember, your partner is in charge of how they ask for time and space. You are in charge of how you hear it.

"SO YOU WANT ME TO BACK OFF?"

"I really don't enjoy this activity. I'd prefer it if you did it by yourself."

KAREEM OWNS TWO HORSES and rides regularly. His wife is afraid of horses and resists getting involved with them. Marilyn enjoys spending Saturdays rummaging through garage sales. She wishes her husband would join her. Fishing is John's big love. His girlfriend is a vegetarian, hates putting worms on a hook, and would rather read a book. Sarah is an avid golfer. She recently asked her partner, "You know I love golf. Why won't you do it with me?"

You and your partner may have a common interest that builds a strong sense of connectedness in your relationship. Perhaps you play bridge together, dance, or jog regularly in the morning. Maybe you go camping every weekend, water ski, or jump out of airplanes holding hands. More power to you. A shared hobby or interest that you both enjoy can bring you closer.

On the other hand, it is not necessary for couples to do everything together in order to be happy. In fact, the reverse may be true. Coercing a common interest may produce tension, resentment, and stress. If that's the case, resist. Tell your partner, "I really don't enjoy this activity. I'd prefer it if you did it by yourself."

You already do many things together. You eat, sleep, have sex, and watch TV together. Maybe you pray together, spend holidays together, and raise children together. Is it really all that important that you take that yoga class together? Is it critical that you both learn how to shoot skeet or attend the dog training sessions?

Giving your partner space and permission to enjoy his horses can create a healthy separateness. Supporting your spouse's desire to fish without your being present is a gift that can benefit both parties. Occasional distance created by a Saturday alone scrounging through other people's junk can bring a renewed interest in your partner when you return home.

Respect each other's differences. See diversity as a strength. Couple when you both enjoy the common activity. Uncouple when one of you lacks interest, patience, or desire. Recouple when the activity is concluded.

HEARING

"I really don't enjoy this activity. I'd prefer it if you did it by yourself" is an honest communication from your partner. Trust it. He or she is telling you that this is an activity that is not important to them. They want you to know that if it is important to you, you have their blessing to continue participating, minus their involvement.

**"This is for me,
not against you."**

JOAN WAS NOT LOOKING FORWARD to the holidays this year. And she didn't know what to do about it.

There were a lot of things Joan enjoyed about the holidays. She loved seeing her children and the grandchildren. She liked having them all spend time at her home. She thoroughly enjoyed the comments they made when they raved about what a good cook she was. She always received positive comments on her turkey and dressing. And the compliments bestowed on her for the homemade pie she made from the cherry tree out back got more appreciative every year. She liked the smiles and giggles that came from her grandchildren when she turned on the old electric train that traveled around the Christmas tree every year. And everyone always enjoyed the lights and other decorations she placed inside and outside her home.

Yes, there were many delights to the holiday season for Joan. But the holidays also meant a considerable amount of work for her. This year she would be doing most of that work alone while her husband worked overtime. It was the effort and energy necessary to prepare for the gathering of her family that weighed heavily on Joan's mind. She didn't want to do all that work this year. She didn't think she was up to it. She toyed with the idea of suggesting that the family Christmas celebration be held at one of her children's homes. But she felt guilty. She thought she would be letting everyone down if she didn't do Christmas as usual.

Joan felt selfish knowing that she didn't want to host the family Christmas. In the past she had ignored her desires and pushed through the frustration of all the preparation. Later, after it was all over, she got angry with herself for not taking better care of herself. Joan needed a piece of Couple Talk to share with her family. But before she used any verbal skills with her husband and family members, she needed to use the same language with herself. At this point the phrase, "This is for me, not against you," is beneficial.

"This is for me, not against you" is a phrase that can be used effectively as self-talk. By using it repetitiously with yourself, you can calm the internal desire to please your partner at your expense. You realize that it is permissible to have desires and that those desires are not designed to harm others but to help yourself.

When the desire to please others at your own expense has been calmed, you can use this phrase aloud with others. These words can then be said in a compassionate way that speaks about what you are for, not about what you are against.

"This is for me, not against you" is language that communicates: I respect your feelings and I'm taking responsibility for my own well-being. It announces to your partner: I support our being individuals within this coupled relationship.

"This is for me, not against you" frees each individual in the relationship to be responsible for themselves. It allows them to take care of their own needs while assuring their partner that his or her needs are also important.

Joan spent three weeks saying, "This is for me, not against you," aloud to herself. She said it sixty times a day. When she felt comfortable she shared her feelings with her spouse and her children.

When Joan finally told her husband how she felt, he said, "I thought you liked putting up the tree and decorations by yourself. That's why I always plan to work more. I do it to stay out of your way." With the new information on the table, and Joan communicating a belief that it was both permissible and desirable to stick up for herself, solution-seeking was the next step. She and her husband created a plan to work around the house together for several evenings. They also decided to cut back on decorating and food preparation. Joan's children agreed to help with the meal preparations, although they requested that she continue the tradition of baking the cherry pie.

If you're the kind of person who is assertive and already stands up for yourself, if you can already say no and put yourself first without feeling guilty, you may not need this piece of Couple Talk.

Joan was a perfect candidate for the phrase, "This is for me, not against you." She had a difficult time saying no or putting her own needs first. Although she displayed co-dependent behaviors and desired to make changes, she struggled with confronting others. Even after her holiday success with this piece of Couple Talk Joan admitted, "It seemed like such an easy thing to say, but it wasn't. The phrase enabled me to be comfortable enough to state my needs aloud." Joan reports that she still says, "This is for me, not against you," to herself from time to time just so she doesn't slip back into thinking that she has to do it all.

HEARING

When you hear your partner say, "This is for me, not against you," know that they are taking care of themselves. They are telling you that what they're doing is not against you. Hear that it's about them. Hear that it's about their specific needs and desire to stand up for themselves.

**"I'm leaving and
I am coming back."**

HAVE YOU EVER BEEN SO ANGRY with your partner that
you just wanted to storm out and slam the door? If so,
you were probably so mad that all you really wanted at
that moment was to get away, clear your head, and be
left alone for a little while. It might not have been a
bad idea.

When you're really angry, you may need to take a
time-out for yourself. At that point it may be wise to
leave in order to keep from saying something you'll
regret later. Leaving is not necessarily good or bad. It's
how you leave that's important.

"I'm leaving and I'm coming back" is Couple Talk
that accompanies a quality exit. It announces three
important things to your partner. First, this sentence
tells them that your feelings are so intense right now
that you need to leave. It communicates that you need
more space than you would gain by simply going to
another room. Escaping the entire situation by leaving
the house is the only way you feel you can get the
break you need.

A second important message this Couple Talk strategy communicates is your intent. It tells your partner you are coming back. If you choose to walk out, for whatever reason, your partner will feel some anxiety, fear, and concern. By delivering this message as you exit, at least they don't have to worry about whether or not you're coming back.

Third, "I'm coming back" speaks to responsibility. It reminds you and your partner that you are going to return and address the situation. It serves to remind each of you that you are both responsible for eventually moving this situation from conflict to resolution.

Your responsibility includes not leaving your partner or the situation hanging. It involves returning in a mood that doesn't feature sulking, stonewalling, anger, or threats. You're leaving now so you can come back later ready to address the situation in a thoughtful, kind, solution-oriented manner.

If you don't talk about the issue and seek a resolution upon your return, then your leaving will have served no other purpose than to escape your feelings and duck conflict. If left unresolved, those feelings will surface again. So will the conflict.

HEARING

When you hear, "I'm leaving and I'm coming back," you can be sure of two things. Number one, your partner is angry. Number two, he or she is coming back. Do not hear, Come after me and help me feel better. Let your partner go. Resist running after them in an attempt to diffuse the situation. He or she will be back.

Hear the deep respect your partner has for your feelings. Remember that in the midst of strong emotion they respected you enough to tell you they were coming back.

CHAPTER 8

The Language
of Autonomy

"How can I be most helpful right now?"

DOROTHY CONSIDERED IT quite an honor to be named chairperson of the annual Women's Conference in her hometown. She took her responsibilities seriously, throwing herself into lining up speakers, structuring a budget, obtaining advertising, creating brochures, handling audiovisual requests, and dealing with all the other tasks that needed to be handled or delegated for this important event. For over a year she planned, organized, and coordinated in a professional and competent manner.

The night before the big event Dorothy had trouble sleeping. Questions raced through her head. Will the main speaker be entertaining and practical? Will the audiovisual equipment function properly? Will the caterers show up on time with the correct amount of food? Will the weather hurt attendance?

During the time she did sleep that night an electrical storm caused a temporary power outage in her home. Because of the power failure Dorothy's alarm clock failed to awaken her at the appropriate time. When she learned the correct time from her radio that morning and realized she was an hour behind schedule, she moved into panic mode.

With no warning or accompanying social ameni-
ties, Dorothy abruptly woke up her husband, Charlie.
After hearing an excited, condensed version of his
wife's predicament, Charlie responded, "How can I be
most helpful right now?"

"How can I be most helpful right now?" were the
words he spoke, but the real message he delivered with
his choice of language was, How can I love and serve
you best in this situation?

"How can I be most helpful?" communicates: I can
see your needs are more important than mine at this
moment. I'm willing to put my needs on the shelf for
now. What is the best way I can help you get through
this crisis?

Notice that Charlie did not immediately spring
into action, telling his wife what to do. He didn't say,
"Calm down, your hysteria will only make things
worse." He didn't begin barking orders, telling each
family member what to do to help Mom get to the
conference in the quickest way possible. He refrained
from using the "I know best" strategy and gently but
lovingly put the problem back on his wife's shoulders
with, "How can I be most helpful?"

Whose problem is this anyway? It is Dorothy's. If
Charlie jumps out of bed and takes over by offering
well-intentioned problem-solving solutions, he robs
his wife of the problem and the opportunity to solve it
herself. If he ignores his wife, tells her to handle it, or
rolls over and goes back to sleep, he misses an opportunity to strengthen the love and connectedness in
their relationship.

By asking, "How can I be most helpful to you?"
Charlie finds that middle ground—the place that
leaves the problem with his wife but also communicates his willingness to help out. His intent is to help
without rescuing. His intent is to serve her agenda, not
his. His desire is to keep off the stage because this is
his wife's drama, her conference, and her problem.

Yet, with his words and his actions, Charlie demonstrates that he is present for her by being willing to help her meet her needs.

A former client of Tom's married a man with a college degree. Since his spouse didn't have the formal education that he had, the husband was quick to offer instant solutions to many of her problems. This created much friction in the relationship. Instant answers were not what this woman needed in order to feel competent, capable, and worthwhile.

"Here's what you need" is language that creates divisiveness in relationships. "What are your needs?" is language that breeds connectedness.

When confronted with, "I had a terrible day. I have a million things to do and not enough time to do them," "I feel like I'm being pulled in several directions," or "It's no use. I'll never get this done in time," refrain from rushing in with solutions. Consider listening. Consider suspending your own agenda. Consider saying, "What's the best thing I can do for you at this moment?" Uttering those words might just be the best thing you can do at that moment.

HEARING

If your partner's words are, "How can I be most helpful right now?" hear that he or she is at your service. Hear that they are willing to do whatever it is that you need done at this moment. Hear also that your partner is not going to take over and solve the problem, fix the situation, or dominate the solution-seeking. They are saying, This is your problem. How do you want me to help?

"Would you like help with that?"

JOSE ENJOYS HELPING OTHERS. He is ever ready to lend a helping hand or offer a suggestion. When he helps others, Jose is even happy to do the task himself. No job seems too big or too small. He will dig a hole, plant flowers, do an Internet search, move the couch, vacuum the floor, wash the car, or get the kids ready for bed.

At first, Carlotta thought her partner's helpful attitude was wonderful. After all, she lived with a man who was willing to help with anything. Two of her best friends were envious and even wished aloud that their husbands could be more like Jose.

After a steady diet of helping, Carlotta began to feel different about it. Eventually, the helping didn't feel like helping any longer. Jose seemed to always have a better idea or a faster way. "Here, grab it this way, it'll be easier," he would say. Or "Let's place it here instead of over there." The helping slowly began to feel like taking over.

When Carlotta wanted to accomplish something by herself, she would begin a task without Jose. As soon as he noticed, Jose would spring into action with, "Let me get that for you," or "I'll lift that for you." "Don't strain yourself," he'd say. "I can do it. Slide over. Let me give it a whirl."

Carlotta didn't want to complain about feeling over-helped. There were many occasions when she really appreciated Jose's help. And she didn't want to screw that up. Yet, tension and resentment were growing in their relationship. Something needed to change.

You may be thinking at this point that Carlotta needs to learn to speak up for herself. Indeed, she could benefit from learning to use language that announces whether or not she would like to have help. A simple, "I'd rather do this by myself," or "I want to feel the satisfaction of accomplishment that goes with doing this task on my own" would be useful. So would an invitation to Jose to join her in solution-seeking on this issue.

Yet it was Jose who took the first step to reduce the relationship tension created in part by his over-functioning. At a Couple Talk seminar at his Fortune 500 Company Jose learned about frequent helpers and how they rob their partners of feelings of accomplishment and personal gratification and of the benefits of struggling with the process. He realized that he did indeed over-function and deprive Carlotta of the sense of ownership that comes from completing a task by oneself.

"Would you like help with that?" is the question Jose learned to ask before jumping up to help. By asking this question he gave Carlotta a choice. He allowed her to determine how much independence she wanted. She was able to decide when, where, and how often she wanted help.

Over time Jose learned that he was actually helping Carlotta both when he helped and when he didn't help. When she did request his help, he did just what was asked—helped without taking over. When she refused help, Jose knew that by backing off he was helping his wife develop the confidence that would come from learning how to do something herself in her own way.

"Would you like some help with that?" is an offer to be the servant, not the master. When you do help, it's important to harness your need to control and let your partner assume the reins. Remember, you are the helper.

HEARING

When you hear, "Would you like help with that?" hear the offer of a choice. You get to decide whether or not you want help. Your partner is respecting your space, ability, knowledge, and independence. He or she is willing to accept your desire to struggle to find the answer, even if they think they already know it.

Hear your partner offering to help, not offering to do it. Remember, the degree of help you accept is up to you. If you don't want any help, say so. If you would like help, say "Yes!" Then tell your partner how he or she could be most helpful.

"Let me know when you're ready to tell me."

MARILYN WAS FEELING DEPRESSED. She noticed it first on Monday, when it appeared as a slight lack of joy. On Tuesday it felt more like a case of the blues. By Wednesday she had created a full-blown depression for herself.

Although Marilyn was keenly aware of her depressed state, she was unsure what had caused it or how she had created it. She suspected it had something to do with the vacation plans that she and her husband, Reginald, had agreed to days earlier. But she wasn't sure.

Marilyn's husband of nineteen years was sensitive to her occasional mood swings. He noticed what he termed, "the blue funk." He had seen it many times before in their years together. Wednesday evening Reginald asked, "Want to talk?"

"Nope," said Marilyn, more unsure of what to talk about than unwilling to talk.

"Sometimes it helps just to start talking," Reginald suggested, attempting to nudge her into conversation one more time.

"Not sure what's going on," Marilyn informed him. "I've been thinking about our trip to Florida next month. I'm not sure exactly what it is. I think I just need some time to be with it for a while."

"Let me know when you're ready to tell me," Reginald replied. He gave Marilyn a wink and blew her a kiss from across the room. Both smiled and returned to what they had been doing.

"Let me know when you're ready to tell me" is Couple Talk that communicates respect. It says, I respect your space as well as your need to have time to think and process. It tells your partner, I respect you enough not to push or attempt to pull it out of you when you're not ready to communicate.

"Let me know when you're ready to tell me" allows. It allows the other person time. It allows the process of marinating to occur. It allows your partner to be in control of when and where to communicate. It allows you to be in charge of you and your partner to be in charge of him- or herself.

Partners do not have to be at the same emotional place at the same time. Neither do they have to be ready to talk at the same time. Use "Let me know when you're ready to tell me" to take the pressure off your partner. It will help prevent them from feeling cornered. It will allow them to relax and come to an understanding of what's going on in their own way at their own time.

Everything doesn't need to be fixed right now or understood in this present moment. This release from the need for instant communication could well enhance the communication process between you and your partner in the long run. Your tolerance of some ambiguity may even help your partner arrive at their own truth more quickly.

"Let me know when you're ready to tell me" is not permission to never tell. It is acknowledgment that your partner may need some time and space right now. It is agreement from both of you that you are coming back to this issue later. It is agreement that you will stand together with an unresolved issue for the time being, but that resolution will ultimately occur.

HEARING

Do not hear, "Let me know when you're ready to tell me," as lack of interest on the part of your partner. Do not hear it as permission to let this issue slide slowly out of sight. Hear instead your partner's interest in the topic as well as his or her respect for your right to decide the timing.

TEN THINGS TO SAY TO PROMOTE AUTONOMY

1. "I respect your right to choose."

2. "If there is any way I can help, let me know."

3. "While you visit the museum I think I'll go shopping."

4. "I enjoy your unique outlook on things. I'm glad we don't see everything the same way."

5. "I'll support you from the sidelines on this one."

6. "Let's compare our goals and see how they're the same and how they're different."

7. "I have needs that are different from yours."

8. "Go on ahead. I'll meet you there."

9. "What role would you like to have in the family?"

10. "Where do you need space right now?"

"ALL RIGHT. I <u>WILL</u> GET MY OWN
SANDWICH. WHERE DO WE
KEEP THEM?"

"Let me struggle with this."

SARAH AND JOE were having a quiet breakfast together at their favorite restaurant. They frequently went for breakfast just to be with one another and talk. On this particular morning they were talking about sex and intimacy.

"I don't feel as if our sex has been very exciting or stimulating lately," Joe began. "You don't seem interested or into it. Is there something up with you?"

After a moment's reflection Sarah responded, "What makes sex exciting for me is how I'm thinking at the moment. Sex starts in my mind. For the past couple of months you seem to have been more focused on the 'act' of sex than on the love that goes with it. I've had trouble getting that out of my mind."

Joe sat for a moment without responding. He was clearly caught off-guard by Sarah's response. When he did speak, he said only, "Let me struggle with that statement for a moment." Sarah honored his request and sat quietly.

After a minute Joe said, "I need a couple of days to think about what you said. Let's talk about something else for now." Sarah replied, "That's OK with me, and this is important so let me know when you're ready to talk about it some more." Joe nodded his agreement. The rest of their breakfast time was spent discussing other topics.

At times your partner will say something that surprises you. When that happens you may need to let it sink in and wrap your thoughts and feelings around it before you respond. That's where, "Let me struggle with this," becomes useful. "Let me struggle with this" will give you the time you need to monitor and process your internal reactions before you jump to conclusions or say something you don't really mean.

"Let me struggle with this for a moment" is also useful when you're sharing your thoughts aloud and don't want your partner to jump in with an answer. By stating, "Let me struggle with this for a few minutes," you announce, I need to hear myself talk about this aloud for awhile. Please just listen to me for a moment.

This Couple Talk sentence clearly states, I want to come up with some answers to this one on my own. Let me struggle. Let me explore my feelings. Let me have the satisfaction of figuring it out myself. With this Couple Talk strategy you are asking your partner to take a step back and let you do the mental and emotional work around the topic or issue at hand.

As you make this statement it is often useful to let your partner know how he or she can help you. You may need them to listen as you talk aloud about the thoughts in your head.

You may need to brainstorm some ideas with your partner. Perhaps you want only a moment or two of silence to collect your thoughts. Or maybe you need a day or two to process the information thoroughly. Whatever it is you need, let your partner know.

In the scenario above, Joe needed a couple of days to process his reaction. What you will need depends on what you're thinking and feeling at that moment. Be specific with your request as to what would be most helpful to you. That will give your partner clear direction concerning the role you would like them to play.

HEARING

If you hear, "Let me struggle with this," as Don't help me, or Leave me alone! you are taking your partner's request for autonomy personally. Be careful. Hearing their request this way could lead to the erroneous conclusion: He [or she] doesn't want me around. That could in turn lead to the defensive response, "You never want my help. You're always excluding me."

Hear this phrase for what it is—a call for a specific type of help. Your partner is asking for assistance. They are saying: Please help me in a different way. Assist me by granting me time to struggle and figure this one out on my own. Support my efforts to understand what is going on here by giving me the space I need.

"I want you to scratch my back."

"I want to go to Mexico for a vacation this year."

"I would like to be alone for a while."

"I want to drive."

"I'd like you to touch me a little harder.
And please don't stop."

"I want to eat out tonight."

"My preference is to see a different movie."

MOST OF US do not live with a psychic. Yet we often act as if we do. We hang onto our wants without verbalizing them and then resent it if our partner doesn't figure them out. We get mad if they don't read our mind.

When wants go unspoken, we activate the myth of "the glass head." No one can see inside our heads. This piece of anatomy is not transparent. Yet, when we do not verbalize wants, we behave as though our significant other can see right through the glass and immediately know what we're thinking. They can't.

Do you ever catch yourself thinking: If he loved me, he'd know? How about: If he really cared, he'd figure it out? Or what about this one: If you don't know, I'm not going to tell you? If so, you've been indulging the myth of the glass head. It might be time to explore the possibility that you're getting angry at your spouse for not automatically knowing what you failed to state aloud.

One way to greatly diminish your chances of getting what you want in life is to fail to verbalize your wants. If you're the only one who knows that you want a back rub, an ice cream sundae, a second orgasm, or time to read the evening paper alone, your odds of getting it are significantly reduced.

Some people don't get what they want in their lives because they're afraid to say "I want." It's easier not to tell and resent than it is to tell and risk rejection. People who don't ask for what they want often fear rejection and prevent themselves from risking further "I wants" by taking rejection personally. They do this by following a rational statement with an illogical conclusion.

For instance, if you say to your partner, "I'd like you to scratch my back," and she replies, "I don't want to," her rational statement is simply, "I don't want to." It's important that you not add onto it the illogical self-talk, She doesn't love me, or I'm not a worthwhile person.

Your partner's statement tells more about her than it does about you. It may mean she's tired. It may mean she's busy. Or it may mean she just doesn't feel like it. Whatever her statement, it is about her. It is not about you. You don't have to take it personally.

Other people don't express wants because they think it's self-centered. "I want" is not the whiny demand of a spoiled child. It is a direct communication from a mature adult who believes in giving their partner important information.

When you share your wants, don't do it with the attitude that you have to get what you want—or that you even expect it. Share your preferences as a way of giving your spouse important information about yourself so you can begin a meaningful dialogue. The approach can be summarized this way: This is what *I* want. Tell me what *you* want, or react to what I want. Then let's talk it over and see if we can reach a consensus.

Do you have some unexpressed wants? Your partner is probably not psychic. Why not share them aloud right now? If you want to, of course.

HEARING

When you hear the words "I want" come out of your partner's mouth, hear what follows as a preference. Hear them asking rather than demanding. Realize that you have a partner who does not expect you to read their mind and who is willing to ask for what he or she wants. Decide whether or not you will grant their wish and inform them as directly and openly as they stated their request.

**"WHAT AM I DOING? I'M STARTING
DINNER LIKE YOU TOLD ME."**

"Watch me."

"OUCH, THAT'S TOO HARD. You're starting to hurt me," Yoko said softly.

"I'm sorry. I thought you liked it that way," her partner whispered back.

"Here, let me show you. Sit back. Watch me," Yoko replied.

Yoko lay back on the bed and began to masturbate while Cathy watched. Yoko described what she was doing and why. Her partner watched intently, taking mental notes. It was arousing for Cathy to watch Yoko masturbate, and she was tempted to join in several times. But Yoko encouraged her to stay in the role of observer and learn from the entire process. When she had finished, Yoko smiled and said, "Now, you show me how you like to be pleased, and I'll watch."

Yoko was skilled at bringing herself to orgasm, but she was also skilled at something else: using effective Couple Talk. She was able to talk about sex, orgasms, and related issues without embarrassment or shame. She was able to articulate to Cathy what she wanted and how she wanted it done. Over time, she and her partner learned a lot about each others' bodies and each others' desires. It is no accident that they enjoy a satisfying sex life.

Yoko and Cathy have different sexual appetites and desires. When they reach climax, one is loud; the other is quiet. One likes to fantasize; the other does not. One likes a soft, steady touch; the other likes to be teased. Both enjoy orgasms and both enjoy pleasing the other.

There is no right way to reach an orgasm. There is only your way and your partner's way. If your partner doesn't know your "right way," don't subject him or her to a guessing game. Show them. If you're unsure of your partner's "right way," don't try to be a psychic. Ask.

Show each other how you like to reach an orgasm or how you like to be touched. Teach each other. Then, when you engage in foreplay, your partner will know what you enjoy and how to do it. With the guesswork gone, the foreplay can turn to pleasing, teasing, adding variation, or focusing on the feeling.

HEARING

When your partner says, "Watch me," don't take it as a criticism. He or she is not telling you what you are doing wrong. They are communicating what they would like. This communication is about them. It is not about you.

Hear, "Watch me," as a gift your partner is giving you. They are offering you an important lesson on how they like to be pleased. Since you want to please them, this is a great opportunity to learn how to do it in ways that will be mutually satisfying.

Hear the incredible amount of trust your partner has in you as evidenced by their sharing of intimate, personal information. Honor it by taking their request seriously and using the information to improve your relationship.

"Shall I rent a mystery or a video with
a happy ending?"

"Do you want me to order Chinese or pizza?"

"Do you want to drive first or second?"

"Shall I do baths or stories?"

"Should I plant another row of corn
or switch to flowers?"

IF ENCOURAGING AUTONOMY in your partner through
shared control is your goal, "You decide" is an effective
response to each of those questions. "You decide" is
Couple Talk language that shares power. It builds
respect and fosters autonomy within the relationship.

Language of this type gives your partner the helm
and allows them the opportunity to guide some decisions that affect both of you. It communicates: I trust
you and your decision-making ability. I accept and
support your decision regardless of what you choose.

"You decide" is not to be used if you have a strong
preference about the topic at hand. In those cases,
share your ideas. Retain the opportunity to have

input in the decisions made. When you want to have a part in the decision-making process, suspend the use of this Couple Talk strategy and work with your partner to arrive at an answer or solution that you can both support.

When you say, "You decide," you are agreeing to not complain or argue later about your partner's decision. This is not a test to see if he or she can guess the right answer. Nor is it a time to make them pay for failing the test. If you hear yourself saying, "You decide," and then complaining and arguing about the decision made, you weren't ready to let your partner decide. Say, "You decide," only when you can loving-ly release the decision and openly accept whatever that decision is.

Some people use "You decide" as a way to avoid taking responsibility or to shift blame. They leave decisions for their partner so they remain free of responsibility. If the decision doesn't work out as planned, the partner is to blame. Playing the blame game creates divisiveness and resentment in rela-tionships. "You decide" is put to better use when it is offered as choice with no hidden agenda.

Are you ready for a relationship that fosters auton-omy and builds respect? Are you ready to share power and control? Are you ready to release decisions to your partner and support them in those decisions? Are you really ready? You decide.

HEARING

Hear "You decide" as your partner's invitation to share in the power and control of the relationship. Hear their desire to share the decision-making responsibilities with you. He or she may be attempting to get you to be more involved. Or perhaps they are simply worn out from a full day and would prefer not to make any more decisions right now. Either way, hear the confidence they have in you to make decisions.

CHAPTER 9

The Language
of
Behavioral Change

"Let's make a
BE choice."

EDGAR AND PAULINE WERE DREADING the upcoming conference with their son's fourth-grade teacher. They had requested the meeting because they objected to the discipline strategies the teacher employed. They felt their son was being unfairly treated and wanted to express their concerns to his teacher face-to-face. As they buckled their seat belts for the short trip to school, Pauline suggested, "Let's make a BE choice."

Jenny and Jerry were on their way to dinner. A sitter was watching the children, and they had several hours before they were expected home. As they pulled into the parking lot of their favorite Italian restaurant, Jerry said, "Let's make a BE choice."

All of us are familiar with DO choices. We make decisions to do laundry, clean the garage, watch television, go to the movies, plan a party. Some of us even create "to do" lists for things we want to remember to do on the weekend, accomplish before we leave on vacation, or complete on a trip across town to the mall. Less often do we make BE choices. A BE choice is a decision we make about how to BE when we DO whatever it is that we do.

For instance, when Jerry and Jenny decided to go out to dinner, that was their DO choice. While they are "doing" that activity, they could choose to BE several different ways. They could choose to BE adventurous and risk eating some new meal that they hadn't yet experienced. They could choose to BE frugal and examine the menu, searching for the best bargain. They could choose to BE friendly. Having made that decision, they might initiate conversations with other couples, smile at the server, and act friendly toward each other.

Whatever BE choice Jerry and Jenny make, that decision will greatly affect their experience of dinner. They will DO dinner regardless of how they choose to BE. But how they experience dinner will vary depending on how they choose to BE.

Edgar and Pauline are on their way to school. They are going to DO a conference with their son's teacher. The flavor, tone, content, and outcome of their meeting will change drastically depending on how they choose to BE during that conference. They may choose to BE confrontational, thorough, efficient, empathetic, sincere, grateful, helpful, disgusted, concerned, open-minded, or one of a variety of other possibilities.

Making a BE choice before they meet with the teacher does not guarantee Edgar and Pauline a particular outcome. They do not control all parts of this equation. They are not in charge of how the teacher thinks, how she will interpret their concern, or how she will respond. Those choices belong to the teacher. One portion of this equation that Edgar and Pauline do get to manage is how to BE in relation to the teacher's reactions. That is their choice.

What making a BE choice in advance accomplishes for Edgar and Pauline in this situation is this: It makes their intention conscious. By thinking about, consciously choosing, and verbalizing a BE choice, they increase the likelihood that they will maintain their chosen posture and not be thrown off by events that transpire once the meeting begins. Verbalizing their BE choice helps them stay awake, alert, and aware of how they want to BE while the event is unfolding.

Being gives birth to doing. If Pauline and Edgar decide to BE excited, it is likely they will DO things that demonstrate excitement. If they decide to BE respectful and stay conscious of that choice, respectful behaviors will surely follow. What they DO will flow out of how they choose to BE.

Are there times when it would serve you and your partner to make a BE choice? How about when you're spending the evening with your in-laws? Could this Couple Talk technique be used as you head upstairs to the bedroom, sit down to work on the family budget, or decide how to handle a discipline strategy with your child? How about when you shop for a new car, go for a walk, or take a three-hour car ride? Perhaps you could even make a BE choice as you read this section aloud and discuss its contents with your partner.

HEARING

When you partner suggests, "Let's make a BE choice," he or she is saying they want to take responsibility for their attitude by consciously choosing it in advance. They're saying that this situation is so important that they don't want to leave attitude to chance. They want to be in control of their stance toward the situation and aren't willing to accept any attitude that might just show up. They are inviting you to join in that process.

"I'd like you to
put down the paper
when I talk to you."

NO COUPLE GOES THROUGH LIFE without being irritated and frustrated with each other on occasion. Differing needs collide. Personalities clash. Hard feelings occur. Conflicts arise. It's called "living together." Learning to express concerns effectively is an important skill for committed couples. We suggest that you communicate your concerns using positive phrasing.

"I'd like you to put down the paper when I talk to you" is an example of positive phrasing. It tells what you want rather than what you don't want. "You never put down the paper when I'm talking" is negative phrasing. It describes the behavior you do not desire. Positive phrasing is generally more effective because it plants the seed for the positive behavior you want to create, it sounds polite, and it communicates respect. It describes what you would like to have happen.

"I want to hear more compliments" is more respectful than "You hardly ever say nice things to me." "I want to have gas in my car" is polite. "You used up all my gas again" is not.

Examine the following comments. Which way would you prefer each concern be shared with you?

"You've been leaving pee on the toilet," or "I need you to make sure the toilet seat is dry when you finish in the bathroom"?

"You said you would put the tools away in the garage and you haven't yet," or "The tools need to be in their places so I can find them when I need them"?

"You never show any affection unless you want sex," or "I need some hugs and kisses that are just hugs and kisses"?

"You always put the kids first," or "I'd like some quality time in the middle of the day"?

Any negative concern can be turned into a positive suggestion. Focus on what you want rather than on what you don't want. Concentrate on the behavior you prefer and say that. Put positive phrasing to work in your relationship today.

Hearing

When you hear a concern expressed with positive phrasing, pay attention. Your partner is working hard to send you clean, descriptive feedback about his or her desires. Seriously consider the message. Regardless of whether or not you choose to respond affirmatively, honor your partner for their effort. They are demonstrating skill in communicating their needs.

"I won't forget your birthday anymore."

"I won't sulk around your mother."

"I won't correct your English in
front of our friends."

"I won't use that word in the presence of
the children again."

ALL OF THOSE COMMENTS were spoken by people with positive intentions. All were attempts to communicate a desire to change a behavior. All could be strengthened by using positive phrasing to change the focus from what *won't* be done to what *will* be done.

"I will remember your birthday from now on" is an example of using positive phrasing to state your intention. It helps clarify the behavior that is desired rather than dwelling on the behavior that is being eliminated. It paints a positive picture of what *will* be done in the minds of both sender and receiver.

"I intend to speak up around your mother, sharing my concerns in a polite manner" tells where you are headed. It communicates direction and focuses on the desired behavior.

When informing your partner of positive intentions, stating what you will do helps turn your positive intentions into positive actions. When you implement the new positive actions, there will no longer be a need for a "won't." Do what you said you will do and the "won't" will take care of itself.

Hearing

If your partner tells you," I won't do that anymore," hear it as a positive intention. Affirm that intention and gently invite them to think about and communicate alternative behaviors by asking, "What *will* you do?" This question is an invitation to your partner to articulate a plan of action that focuses on the positive.

EVERYONE MAKES MISTAKES. When we're fatigued, stressed, or uninformed, we do and say things that are unskilled. We all engage in behaviors and use words we wish we hadn't. At these times an important piece of Couple Talk is needed.

If you overreact, snap at your partner, or exhibit any behavior you wish you could take back, don't allow hurtful feelings and resentment to fester. Use Couple Talk to build the connectedness and trust that are necessary for maintaining a loving relationship. An apology is in order.

It probably doesn't surprise you that we suggest an apology at times like these. It may surprise you, however, that we recommend you refrain from using the words, "I'm sorry."

"I'm sorry" is an easy way out. It's a simple penance which excuses you from considering a change in your behavior. You don't have to create plans for more appropriate behavior or think about how to behave differently in the future. In fact, you don't have to think at all. You only need to say, "I'm sorry."

Anybody can say, "I'm sorry." You don't even have to mean it. Just say, "I'm sorry," and the issue has been put to rest. It's over.

No. "I'm sorry" isn't good enough. Not if a growing, caring, loving relationship is your goal. If you said or did something you regret, issue an apology. But send that apology with Couple Talk skills that explain what you really meant or describe what you wish you had said or done.

"I made a mistake, Shannon. I was angry and I allowed my temper to get in the way. I love you and I wish I hadn't used those words. What I'd like to have said is, 'I feel frustrated when I come home and there is no note telling me where you are or when you'll be back.'"

Another useful way to apologize is to tell your partner what you learned and what you intend to do differently next time. "I learned you don't like it if I fix myself something to eat without asking you if you'd like something. Next time, I intend to ask if I can fix something for you, too."

Being sorry means being willing to do it differently next time. Telling your partner, "I'm sorry," is easy. Demonstrating that you're sorry is more difficult. If you are really sorry, apologize and then choose behavior that is congruent with your words.

HEARING

Hear, "I'm sorry," as an incomplete sentence. Wait for more. If your partner says, "I'm sorry," and ends the sentence there, invite them to continue with, "Say some more," "What are you sorry about?" or "Please explain to me why you're sorry."

"ARE YOU SURE THAT'S ALL YOU HAVE TO SAY?"

"You can demonstrate that by ..."

CAROL TOOK A RISK at the party. She revealed to her friends her secret goal of winning a blue ribbon for riding her horse. Her husband laughed. Carol flushed and swallowed the bitter retort that instantly formed in her mind.

On the ride home, Carol created personal clarity about her concern. She knew from her Couple Talk training that she needed to get specific with her communication. Telling her husband she felt disrespected would have more meaning if she could clearly state the behavior that bothered her. "I felt disrespected when you laughed when I shared my blue ribbon dream" were the words that formed in her mind.

Carol then took her planning to a higher level. She had learned in the Couple Talk training that getting specific in her communication required more than coming up with a concrete complaint. It also involved creating a concrete positive suggestion—a specific, helpful alternative.

While her husband drove and listened to the radio, seemingly oblivious to his wife's concern, Carol constructed this statement: "When I share a goal in public, please give me your respect. You can demonstrate that by saying something like, 'Carol loves her horse and they're working hard every week toward that goal of a blue ribbon.'"

By the time her husband pulled their car into the driveway, Carol was prepared. Shortly after their arrival home, in the privacy of their living room, she initiated a discussion.

"I felt disrespected when you laughed when I shared my blue ribbon dream tonight," she began. Her husband gave her his full attention. She continued, "When I share a goal in public, please give me your respect. You can demonstrate that by saying something like, 'Carol loves her horse and they're working hard every week toward that goal of a blue ribbon.' I would really appreciate that kind of a response from you."

An hour-long discussion followed. Hugs and kisses marked the end of the discussion. Neither person went to bed angry that night. Neither had trouble getting to sleep. Neither was chewing on anything left unsaid. Closeness prevailed because Carol skillfully used the Couple Talk technique of sharing a concrete positive suggestion.

If your specific complaint is, "When I suggested we go to the movies tonight, you didn't give me a response one way or the other," add a concrete positive suggestion. Include, "When I make a suggestion I like to feel that you heard me. You can demonstrate that by giving me a verbal response—something like, 'I'm too tired tonight' or 'What's showing?'"

When your concrete gripe is, "When you don't tell me I'm the prettiest girl at the dance I start to wonder if you still love me," add a positive suggestion such as, "I want to feel loved and appreciated. You can demonstrate that by whispering in my ear things like, 'You still turn me on' or 'I sure am lucky to be the one taking you home tonight.'"

Concrete behavioral suggestions are just that—suggestions. They are recommendations that could serve as prescriptions for the complaint. They are designed to plant positive ideas in your partner's head and to get them thinking of positive prescriptive possibilities. Suggestions are always framed as positive ideas to increase desired behaviors rather than negative suggestions to decrease unwanted behaviors.

Leave the specific remedy up to your partner. Communicating your concern as skillfully as possible is your choice. How or if they respond is their choice.

HEARING

Hear, "You can demonstrate that by . . . ," as a suggestion. It is intended to get you thinking, to get you engaged in sorting through possibilities and coming up with your own unique ways to remedy the situation.

Yes, it is OK to use the positive suggestion offered by your partner exactly as it was stated. Or feel free to substitute a similar one of your own. Either way, he or she will feel heard and loved, and connectedness will increase.

"Trust me."

JUAN AND JULIA HAD BEEN TOGETHER for 18 years. During that time Julia often gave her attention to other men. Juan called it flirting and frequently expressed his discomfort to Julia. "Oh, I'm just playing around," she told him. "Don't worry about it. Trust me."

Juan did trust Julia, for many years. He trusted her right up until the time he found out about her affair. "I don't think I'll ever trust anyone again," Juan told his counselor. "And certainly not if they tell me to," he added.

If you hear yourself or your partner say, "Trust me," consider it a red flag. If one of you feels a need to use those words, something may not be right concerning your relationship.

> "I'll be there to pick up the kids at seven o'clock. Trust me."

> "I'll invest our money wisely. Trust me."

> "The kitchen will be redone in time for the graduation party. You can trust me."

"I know cars. I've never bought a lemon.
You can trust my judgment."

To say "Trust me" is an indication that you feel a need to convince your partner that you are trustworthy. Why is that so? Is there something in your behavior that indicates you cannot be trusted? Or, as Juan was, has your partner been "burned" and is now finding it difficult to trust?

If you hear yourself saying, "Trust me," take time to examine your relationship. Explore two possibilities.

First, is there something you're doing that demonstrates you are not trustworthy? Ask yourself: Why do I feel that I need to say, "Trust me"? Explore the possibility that you could be choosing a behavior that is giving your partner the impression that you cannot be fully trusted.

Second, if the issue of trust appears to be a particular mindset of your partner based on previous experience, then the words "Trust me" are not the solution. Saying "Trust me" won't change your partner's point of view. Not if he or she has difficulty trusting. The remedy to this type of trust issue can be found in your actions and behaviors.

Trust develops when a person's words are supported by actions. When you say what you are going to do and then you do it, trust grows and is strengthened. The more your actions match your words, the more trust others have in you. The main idea is to stop saying, "Trust me," and start living it instead.

Time plays a role in the development and strengthening of trust. The more opportunities you have to demonstrate how your words and actions flow together, the stronger trust becomes. In the end it is your behavior that should tell your partner, *I can be trusted*. When your behavior sends that message, your words won't have to.

HEARING

When you hear, "Trust me," be cautious. Ask yourself why your partner feels the need to say this to you. Is he or she attempting to help you appreciate that their behavior is demonstrating trustworthiness? If so, could you be missing how their words and actions flow together? Do you have difficulty trusting even when your partner's behavior shows that they are, in fact, trustworthy?

Or are your partner's words incongruent with their behavior? If so, their using the phrase, "Trust me," may be an attempt to cover up and deflect attention from behavior that is less than trustworthy.

When you hear, "Trust me," know that something is amiss. Time invested determining why your partner feels the need to use those words is one way you can together build the necessary trust so that no one will feel the need to say, "Trust me."

"I promise I'll make it up to you."

"I'll meet you there at ten o'clock. I promise."

"I promise I'll put it away."

"I won't do that again. I promise."

"I'll get it done. I promise."

"I promise I'll come back."

"I promise I'll love you forever."

REMOVE "I PROMISE" from those statements and they remain strong.

"I'll make it up to you."

"I'll meet you there at ten."

"I'll put it away."

The words "I promise" are not what give a statement its strength. What gives power and credibility to your words are the actions that follow. Demonstrate your commitment to your words through action. It is the history of your behavior that supports the statements you make. When your actions follow what you say, those actions have more meaning than the words, "I promise."

Do you feel compelled to say, "I promise," to your partner? If so, ask yourself: Why do I need to reinforce my statement with a promise? Look closely at your behavior. Is there something you're doing, or failing to do, that demonstrates you might not follow through with what you say? Do you tell your partner what you are going to do and then fail to follow through? Do you need the words "I promise" to commit yourself to action? Perhaps you are saying, "I promise," for yourself and not for your partner.

Your partner does not need to *hear* "I promise." They need to see your words backed up by action.

HEARING

When your partner uses the words, "I promise," hear his or her struggle to find the drive to follow through. Help them out. Gently and lovingly inform them there is no need for a promise. Remind them that your need is only for completion. Let your partner know that you hear their statement and you believe in their ability to follow through without the promise. Communicate that you appreciate their sharing what they are going to do and that you value their commitment to the action.

"I'll try."

"I'm trying to lose weight."

"I know I have a temper. I'll try to
keep it under control."

"Yes, I'll try to quit smoking."

"I'm trying to be more positive."

"I'll try harder to be nice to your father."

"It's not easy to stop drinking. I'm trying
as hard as I can."

"Let's try to be nice to each other."

"I'll try if you will."

"Hey, don't bug me. I'm trying."

TRYING DOESN'T WORK. Doing does. Anyone busy trying is someone who is not busy doing. In *Star Wars*,
Yoda said, "Do or do not. There is no try." Yoda should
know. He's a Jedi Master, and it takes three hundred
years to become a Jedi Master.

People who are serious about their commitment to change do not use the word "try." They don't talk that way. They say what they are going to do and back it up with behaviors that are congruent with their words.

When you say you are going to TRY, you sabotage your efforts. TRY language creates a picture in your mind of missing the mark and not achieving your stated goal. It gives you an out. After all, if you don't make it, you can always say, "I tried."

If you think trying is helpful, we challenge you the next time you go in for major surgery to imagine the doctor coming in the night before to psyche you up and prep you for the morning operation. As she's preparing you physically, emotionally, and mentally, you ask, "Doc, you're going to be able to pull this off tomorrow, right?" And she answers, "I'm not really sure, but I'm going to try." We don't know about you, but we're getting a new doctor.

A high school counselor attending one of our educator workshops recently told us, "In my business, the word 'try' is a red flag word. Every time I hear a student use it, I know I have no commitment. Yesterday I was working with a high school senior who had already accumulated five tardies to his third-hour class. I asked him what he was going to do about it. He replied, 'I'm going to try harder to get there on time.' I told him I don't accept the word 'try' and pushed him to tell me something he would do differently to make sure he arrived before the bell. He said, 'I told you. I'm going to try really hard to be on time.' I told him again TRYING wasn't good enough and that he would have to come up with some specific behavior that he intended to do differently. I pushed him to articulate a plan of action. After two more attempts to tell me how hard he would TRY, he finally created a plan of taking 2nd and 3rd hour books with him to his 2nd hour class so he wouldn't have to come all the way back to his locker between the two classes. Now he has a chance to be successful. TRYING never works."

Instead of telling your partner you're trying, give specific examples or data. Are you trying to lose weight? What proof do you have? Are you trying to quit smoking? Is there real evidence or is your statement a cop-out?

When you hear yourself use the word TRY, ask yourself: How do I know? Am I controlling my temper or aren't I? Am I being more positive or not? What evidence can I point to? Acknowledge exactly where you are behaviorally on the issue in your own mind first. Then, if you choose, communicate the descriptive, specific proof to your partner.

HEARING

If your partner tells you he or she is going to TRY, chances are whatever it is they are trying to achieve will not happen. If they say they're trying, you know they are not there yet. Ask them to be honest about the results they've created at this point and to communicate those specific results to you without the use of the word "try."

"You don't respect me."

"You don't notice me."

"You're not attracted to me anymore."

"You don't treat me like you love me."

THIS KIND OF COMPLAINING doesn't work. It is ineffective primarily because it is nonspecific. The nebulous format of this style of communication fails to give your partner specific information. It is laced with inferences and judgments and is open to interpretation.

What do you mean when you say, "You don't respect me?" Does that mean your partner doesn't stand up when you enter the room? Does it mean he doesn't hold doors open for you? Does it mean she fails to consult you before she makes major purchases? Or does it mean he or she doesn't use your ideas and suggestions?

Respect means different things to different people. What do *you* mean by it? Get specific in your Couple Talk. If you have a complaint, express it in specific, behavioral terms.

"When I told everyone at the party that my goal was to win a blue ribbon for riding my horse, you laughed at me" is specific. It gives your partner useful information free of inferences. It offers him something concrete he can deal with. It communicates a behavior you do not appreciate rather than infers a general concept such as "lack of respect."

"When I suggested we go to the movies tonight, you didn't give me a response one way or the other" is more specific than "You don't notice me." "You don't tell me I'm the prettiest girl at the dance anymore" is more concrete than "You don't act like you love me." "You didn't ask my opinion on the job offer" is less cloudy than "You don't value me."

Everyone has gripes. Everyone has complaints. You get to express yours. To do that effectively, we suggest you communicate those complaints and gripes with Couple Talk that verbalizes specific behaviors.

Hearing

When your partner says, "You don't value me," know there is a specific incident behind the generalization. Ask about it. Inquire as to how your partner came to that conclusion. Ask for a specific example. Respond to the example rather than to the inference. Your behavior and your partner's feelings are what are important. Concentrate on what you can learn from the behavior that is cited and from observing how that kind of behavior affects your partner's feelings.

"I'm past that."

"That was then. This is now."

"That's not who I am today."

"I don't do that anymore."

"You're thinking of the old me."

"I'm not like that anymore."

THERE ARE TIMES when you know you have changed a pattern and your partner doesn't quite believe it yet. In those instances, their words and behavior indicate that they still think of you as the way you used to be. Their reaction focuses on the "old" you and attempts to contain you in a time and place that you have long since left. That's when "I'm more than that now" becomes useful.

Only use, "I'm more than that now," when you have truly changed. It is only effective if you have a behavioral track record that backs it up. If you do, you can use this style of Couple Talk to remind your partner of your new history. If you have demonstrated a changed attitude through consistent behavior and your partner brings up the past, "I'm more than that now" can serve as a gentle reminder that that was then and this is now.

"I'm more than that now" invites your partner to see you for who you are today. It asks him or her to acknowledge the changes and the efforts you have made. You are calling upon them to reconnect with you and your present behavior.

For "I'm more than that now" to be effective, it must involve more than words. When change in behavior doesn't precede the use of this Couple Talk phrase, more mistrust can occur. Respect for the partnership will diminish.

"I'm more than that now" is not to be used as a retort concerning a behavior you chose last week but want your partner to know you are not doing this week. This communication technique is to be used with a behavior you have eliminated for several months. It should be used to talk about a change that has already taken place, not one that you're hoping to make soon.

Consider Tony and Jan. Upon entering marriage counseling, Tony's major complaint was, "Jan frequently reminds me about a one-night stand I had when we were dating. The incident occurred before we were even married. Since we've been married I have been loyal and true. I get no credit for being faithful for ten years."

Jan's response was to agree that Tony had indeed been faithful since their wedding day, but added, "You flirt every chance you get. You stare at other women. You make sexual comments about what you'd like to do to them. When you act like that I keep thinking that we're only one fight away from your having another affair."

Tony used several "That's not who I am today" messages to tell Jan that his behavior had changed and that he didn't appreciate hearing about the past. But had his behavior really changed? Even though his interest in other women didn't result in sexual contact, his behavior seemed to demonstrate a similar attitude with women.

To Jan, Tony's commitment to her was in question. She saw no change in Tony's level of respect for her, nor any behavioral change that would demonstrate it. On the other hand, Tony thought Jan was being overly sensitive and reading into the situation something that was not really there.

Tony and Jan invested time in marital therapy exploring their commitment to their relationship. They examined their level of respect and caring for each other and the degree of intimacy they desired. They learned over time to make changes in their behavior that demonstrated more clearly how they felt toward one another.

As time passed and the behavior change continued, Tony and Jan found they could both honestly say, "We're more than that now."

HEARING

When you hear, "I'm more than that now," you may be missing the change your partner is making. You may be focusing too much on the past. Check to make sure that you're not being overly sensitive to the issue being raised.

Create a dialogue around the different points of view that are present in your relationship. Maybe your partner's behavior hasn't fully changed but is heading in the preferred direction. Maybe they desire and deserve acknowledgment for their effort to change.

Perhaps you were hoping for change of a different sort. If so, openly discuss where your relationship has been, where it is now, and where you both would like it to be. Through discussion you can identify new behavior changes that can be made individually and collectively.

"I don't want to
do this anymore."

WHEN JOHN SHOWED UP alone for an introductory
Couple Talk presentation, he had been married for
eleven years. He related that he had been fighting
with his wife, Patty, off and on since day one. John
wasn't happy with the results of their arguments,
which included days of silence, walking on eggshells,
ignoring certain topics, stuffing feelings, name-
calling, accusations, and threats of leaving.

As a result of the frequent arguing, John wasn't
enjoying his life with Patty. He had no idea what to
do about the arguing, but of one thing he was certain:
he didn't want to continue in the relationship the way
it was.

At the Couple Talk presentation, John was introduced to the phrase, "I don't want to do this anymore."
He learned that saying, "I don't want to do this anymore," didn't mean he had to leave the relationship.
It could mean:

"I don't want to fight like this anymore."

"I don't want to solve problems
like this anymore."

"I don't want to be treated like this anymore."

"Having all these bills in the drawer is more
than I can stand. I can't do it anymore."

"It seems like we always focus on the negative.
I don't want to do that anymore."

"Yelling at each other is so disrespectful.
I don't want to do this anymore."

John headed home from the seminar that evening
with what he thought was the perfect lead-in for sharing his frustration with Patty. He would use, "I don't
want to do this anymore," as a way of asking her to join
him in searching for a solution to end a situation that
had become intolerable.

John did use the Couple Talk strategy he learned
that night, which initiated a serious dialogue with
Patty, and the next day they called a counselor to set
up an appointment.

"I don't want to do this anymore" can be used to
communicate to your partner when you have reached
the end of the line on an important issue. Perhaps you
have talked all the Couple Talk possible, attempted to
address your concerns in every way you know how,
used all the tools in your toolbox, and still there is
no change in your relationship. Now you need to be
clear with your partner about your refusal to do business as usual.

"I don't want to do this anymore" is a call for a
change. It communicates: *Things need to change between
us.* It is Couple Talk to be used when you are seriously
ready to make a change regardless of what your partner chooses to do.

Maybe you've had enough of the fighting and are
not prepared to leave. Then you say, "I don't want to
do this anymore. I'm done fighting like this. We need
to go to marriage counseling." Maybe you present a

choice for your partner to consider. "I can't do this anymore. We either work on being together or we work on being apart."

"I don't want to do this anymore" and its variations are about being done with the way things currently are. You could be done with the way the finances are being handled, the way the children are being disciplined, or the lack of communication in your relationship. If you have had enough, no matter what it is, then communicate your intentions to change by saying, "I don't want to do this anymore."

"I don't want to do this anymore" is not a threat and should not be used as one. This is not an ultimatum that implies, Do this or else. When you use this phrase you are calling for change and communicating your unwillingness to keep on keeping on.

Your partner can join you in the change or not. That's their choice. Their response to your statement and to the changes you make will give you valuable information about the relationship that you can use in determining your next step.

Perhaps you will get to the point where you have had enough of being in relationship with your partner and decide to end it. You realize you are prepared to file for a divorce or break your pledge of commitment. In that case, "I don't want to do this anymore" is not enough. Say instead, "I don't want to do this anymore. I'm leaving you."

Hearing

Your partner is calling for a change. This could be that final wake-up call, the last warning you're going to get. It could be the beginning of the end of your relationship.

When you hear, "I don't want to do this anymore," get ready for a change. The status quo has ended. You either need to change how you plan to stay together or create a plan for how you intend to separate.

"Will you join me
in counseling?"

IT IS OUR HOPE and belief that if you use the strategies presented in this book and apply them with love and an open heart, neither you nor your partner will ever need to use the words, "Will you join me in counseling?" If you learn these strategies and apply them regularly, you should be able to handle most relationship problems which surface by yourselves. A book, however, has its limits. And so do you. In certain situations you may feel the need to seek the assistance of a professional counselor or therapist. That's what happened to John Marker.

John was a pragmatic kind of guy, and he knew the scope and limits of his abilities. If he had trouble with plumbing he called a plumber. If his car broke down he took it to a mechanic. If his computer didn't respond he called the 800 number that connected him to technical assistance. In short, he asked for help.

After a frustrating year of attempting to work things out with his wife, John asked her, "Melodie, will you join me in counseling?" She consented and they began a new journey together, one designed to move their relationship to a new and exciting level.

John and Melodie knew there was no shame in going to counseling. They did not feel like failures when their relationship broke down anymore than they would have if one of their bodies had broken down. If Melodie had heart problems, she would have gone to a heart doctor. If John developed diabetes, he would have requested help from his physician. So when problems persisted in their marriage, they got help.

"Will you join me in counseling?" invites your partner to come and journey with you. It lets him or her know that you view the current situation as extremely serious. It also tells them that you still care enough about the relationship to want to fix it.

When and how you arrive at the point where you seek professional help is up to you. The following guidelines may be helpful.

Consider joint counseling when:

1. One of you seems to have given up.

2. One or both of you have difficulty discussing neutral subjects without it ending in a fight.

3. One of you is afraid to share emotions because you can't control the outcome.

4. Fights are continually left unresolved.

5. You are using the strategies presented in this book and you don't seem to be getting anywhere.

6. Basic problems exist that are not altered by effective communication.

7. You feel you both need to see things from a third perspective.

8. One or both of you need to feel protected by a referee.

9. One or both of you need to be confronted, but not by each other.

10. One or both of you internalize problems rather than talking about them.

"Will you join me in counseling?" is an invitation to make a commitment—to make one more strong effort on behalf of your relationship. It is an invitation to be honest, to work hard, and to apply what you learn on a regular basis.

In the end, if you choose to end your relationship, a counselor can help you do that cleanly, with integrity and mutual respect. Done this way you will have as few leftover issues and regrets as possible. You will achieve closure.

HEARING

Hear, "Will you join me in counseling?" as a sign that your relationship is not dead. It may be barely breathing, but it is still alive. Your partner is inviting you to join them in an attempt to resuscitate a partnership that is on the way down.

Hear the question as a signal that this is a serious moment. Hear it as a "take stock" time in your relationship and in your life. Hear it as a wake-up call. Hear it as a warning. And hear that there is still enough love there for your partner to ask, "Will you join me in counseling?"

ABOUT THE AUTHORS

CHICK MOORMAN

CHICK MOORMAN IS THE DIRECTOR of the Institute for Personal Power, a consulting firm dedicated to providing high quality professional development activities for educators and parents.

He is a former classroom teacher with over 38 years of experience in the field of education. His mission is to help people experience a greater sense of personal power in their lives so they can in turn empower others.

Chick conducts full-day workshops and seminars for school districts and parent groups. He also delivers keynote addresses for local, state, and national conferences.

He is available for the following topic areas:

FOR EDUCATORS

Achievement Motivation and Behavior
Management through Effective Teacher Talk

Teaching Respect and Responsibility

Improving Student Self-Esteem

Stamping Out Learned Helplessness

Cooperative Learning

Celebrate the Spirit Whisperers

Dealing with Reluctant Learners

FOR PARENTS

Parent Talk: Words That Empower,
Words That Wound

Raising Your Child's Self-Esteem

Building Family Solidarity

Raising Response-Able Children

Grace-Full Parenting

If you would like more information about these programs or would like to discuss a possible training or speaking date, please contact:

Chick Moorman
P.O. Box 547
Merrill, MI 48637
Telephone: (877) 360-1477
Fax: (989) 643-5156
E-mail: ipp57@aol.com
Web site: www.chickmoorman.com

THOMAS B. HALLER,

M.DIV., MSW, ACSW

THOMAS CURRENTLY WORKS in private practice at Shinedling, Shinedling, and Haller, P.C., in Bay City, Michigan, as a child, adolescent and couples therapist; an individual psychotherapist working with individuals; and a chronic pain counselor. He is a certified EEG biofeedback technician, an AASECT certified sex therapist-diplomate, and a certified sports counselor. Thomas has extensive training in psychotherapy with children and couples from the University of Michigan, where he received his Master of Social Work degree. He also is an ordained Lutheran minister with a Master of Divinity degree from Concordia Theological Seminary.

Thomas is a widely sought-after national and international presenter in the areas of parenting, interpersonal relationships, and dealing with chronic pain. He is also the founder and director of Healing Minds Institute, a center devoted to teaching others to focus on and enhance the health of the mind, body, and spirit.

Thomas enjoys weightlifting, soccer, and maintaining the family's horse ranch. He is married with two children. His wife, Valerie, is an Early Childhood educator who teaches kindergarten in the Bay City Public Schools. Valerie enjoys horseback riding, tending to her two horses, and reading with their two boys: Reese, age 6, and Parker, age 3.

Thomas conducts workshops and seminars for churches, school districts, parent groups, and counseling agencies. He is also a regular lecturer at universities across the country.

He is available for the following topic areas:

FOR COUPLES

The Balance of Autonomy and Boundaries

How to Talk to Your Partner About Sex

How to Talk to Your Partner in Language
That Builds Mutual Respect and Intimacy

The Language of Feelings in
Committed Relationships

Response-Able Partnering

FOR PARENTS

The Parent Talk Experience

How to Talk to Your Children About Sex

Creating a Caring Environment in the Home

Managing Aggression and Anger in Children

Understanding Your Children's Feelings

FOR EDUCATORS

Brain Functioning and Behavior in Children

Transforming Aggression in Children

Creating a Caring Environment in the Classroom

Understanding Asperger's Syndrome

You can contact Thomas at:

Shinedling, Shinedling, and Haller, P.C.
2355½ Delta Rd.
Bay City, MI 48706
Telephone: (989) 667-5654
Fax: (989) 667-5330
E-mail: tbhaller@hotmail.com

OTHER BOOKS AND PRODUCTS

SPIRIT WHISPERERS: *Teachers Who Nourish A Child's Spirit,* by Chick Moorman ($25.00)

PARENT TALK: *How to Talk to Your Children in Language That Builds Self-Esteem and Encourages Responsibility,* by Chick Moorman ($13.00)

TEACHER TALK: *What It Really Means,* by Chick Moorman and Nancy Weber ($13.00)

WHERE THE HEART IS: *Stories of Home and Family,* by Chick Moorman ($15.00)

TALK SENSE TO YOURSELF: *The Language of Personal Power,* by Chick Moorman ($13.00)

OUR CLASSROOM: *We Can Learn Together,* by Chick Moorman and Dee Dishon ($20.00)

THE LANGUAGE OF RESPONSE-ABLE PARENTING. Audio cassette tape series featuring Chick Moorman ($39.95)

PARENT TALK FOCUS CARDS, by Chick Moorman ($10.00)

THE PARENT TALK SYSTEM: *The Language of Response-Able Parenting.* Facilitator's Manual by Chick Moorman, Sarah Knapp and Judith Minton ($300.00)

REDUCING FAMILY CONFLICT *Through Effective Parent Talk.* Video tape featuring Chick Moorman ($30.00)